Remember Their Sin No More?

Remember Their Sin No More?

Forgiveness and the Hebrew Bible

Edited by

David J. Shepherd
and Richard S. Briggs

PICKWICK *Publications* · Eugene, Oregon

Pickwick Publications
An Imprint of Wipf and Stock Publishers
199 W. 8th Ave., Suite 3
Eugene, OR 97401

www.wipfandstock.com

PAPERBACK ISBN: 978-1-7252-8196-7
HARDCOVER ISBN: 978-1-7252-8197-4
EBOOK ISBN: 978-1-7252-8198-1

Cataloguing-in-Publication data:

Names: Shepherd, David J. [editor] | Briggs, Richard S., 1966– [editor]

Title: Remember their sin no more? : forgiveness and the Hebrew Bible / edited by David J. Shepherd and Richard S. Briggs.

Description: Eugene, OR: Pickwick Publications, 2022 | Includes bibliographical references and index.

Identifiers: ISBN 978-1-7252-8196-7 (paperback) | ISBN 978-1-7252-8197-4 (hardcover) | ISBN 978-1-7252-8198-1 (ebook)

Subjects: LCSH: Forgiveness of sin—Biblical teaching | Sin—Biblical teaching | Forgiveness—Religious aspects | Bible—Old Testament—Theology

Classification: BS680.F64 S44 2022 (print) | BS680.F64 (ebook)

09/16/22

Permissions

Contents

Contributors

Anthony Bash, St. Giles Church, Durham; Honorary Professor in the Department of Theology and Religion, Durham University, UK; Senior Case Manager, Student Conduct Office, Durham University, UK

Richard S. Briggs, Prior of the Community of St. Cuthbert, St. Nics Church, Durham; Visiting Research Fellow in Old Testament, Cranmer Hall, St. John's College, Durham University, UK

David G. Firth, Old Testament Tutor and Academic Dean, Trinity College, Bristol, UK; Research Associate, University of the Free State, South Africa

Vincenz Heereman, LC, PhD Candidate, University of Notre Dame, USA

J. Gordon McConville, Professor Emeritus in Old Testament Theology, University of Gloucestershire, UK

David J. Reimer, Academic Dean of Faith Mission Bible College, Edinburgh; Honorary Senior Lecturer in the School of Divinity, University of St. Andrews, UK

David J. Shepherd, Associate Professor in Hebrew Bible/Old Testament, School of Religion, Theology, and Peace Studies, Trinity College Dublin, Ireland

J. Michael Thigpen, Provost, Executive Vice President, and Professor of Old Testament, Phoenix Seminary, USA

Abbreviations

AB	Anchor Bible
ABR	*Australian Biblical Review*
ANE	Ancient Near East
AOAT	Alter Orient und Altes Testament
ApOTC	Apollos Old Testament Commentary
ASOR	American Schools of Oriental Research
ATD	Das Alte Testament Deutsch
AV	Authorized Version
BDB	*A Hebrew and English Lexicon of the Old Testament*. Edited by F. Brown et al. Oxford, UK: Clarendon, 1907.
BETL	Bibliotheca Ephemeridum Theologicarum Lovaniensium
BHS	*Biblia Hebraica Stuttgartensia*. Edited by Karl Elliger and Wilhelm Rudolph. Stuttgart: Deutsche Bibelgesellschaft, 1983.
BibInt	*Biblical Interpretation*
BKAT	Biblischer Kommentar, Altes Testament
BSac	*Bibliotheca Sacra*
CBET	Contributions to Biblical Exegesis and Theology

Abbreviations

CBQ	*Catholic Biblical Quarterly*
ConcC	Concordia Commentary
CoS	*Context of Scripture.* 4 vols. Edited by W. W. Hallo and K. L. Younger. Leiden, Neth.: Brill, 1997–2016.
ECC	Eerdmans Critical Commentary
ESV	English Standard Version
FAT	Forschungen zum Alten Testament
FOTL	Forms of the Old Testament Literature
GKC	Gesenius, Wilhelm. *Gesenius' Hebrew Grammar.* Edited by E. Kautzsch, revised by A. E. Cowley. Oxford: Clarendon, 1910.
HALOT	*The Hebrew and Aramaic Lexicon of the Old Testament.* Edited by L. Koehler et al. 4 vols. Leiden, Neth.: Brill, 1994–1999.
HCOT	Historical Commentary on the Old Testament
HKAT	Handkommentar zum Alten Testament
HS	*Hebrew Studies*
HTR	*Harvard Theological Review*
ICC	International Critical Commentary
IECOT	International Exegetical Commentary on the Old Testament
JBL	*Journal of Biblical Literature*
JPS	Jewish Publication Society
JSOT	*Journal for the Study of the Old Testament*
JSOTSup	Journal for the Study of the Old Testament Supplement Series
KJV	King James Version
LHBOTS	The Library of Hebrew Bible/Old Testament Studies
LXX	Septuagint
MT	Masoretic Text
NAC	New American Commentary
NICOT	New International Commentary on the Old Testament

NIDOTTE	*New International Dictionary of Old Testament Theology and Exegesis.* Edited by Willem A. VanGemeren. 5 vols. Grand Rapids: Zondervan, 1997.
NIV	New International Version
NJB	New Jerusalem Bible
NRSV	New Revised Standard Version
OBO	Orbis Biblicus et Orientalis
OTL	Old Testament Library
RB	*Revue biblique*
RBS	Resources for Biblical Study
RevExp	*Review and Expositor*
RSV	Revised Standard Version
SAACT	State Archives of Assyria Cuneiform Texts
SJOT	*Scandinavian Journal of the Old Testament*
SubBi	Subsidia Biblica
TDOT	*Theological Dictionary of the Old Testament.* Edited by G. Johannes Botterweck and Helmer Ringgren. Translated by John T. Willis et al. 18 vols. Grand Rapids: Eerdmans, 1974–2006.
TOTC	Tyndale Old Testament Commentaries
TynBul	*Tyndale Bulletin*
VT	*Vetus Testamentum*
VTSup	Supplements to Vetus Testamentum
WBC	Word Biblical Commentary
WC	Westminster Commentaries
ZAR	*Zeitschrift für altorientalische und biblische Rechtsgeschichte*

Finding Forgiveness in the Hebrew Bible

DAVID J. SHEPHERD

WHILE THE ANCIENT JEWISH sage Ben Sira has much to say about forgiveness (e.g., Sir 5:5; 16:11; 17:29; 18:12; 28:2; 35:3), one of his more intriguing turns of phrase suggests that forgiveness is something which may be "found" (18:20). Because his main point is to encourage his reader to search (i.e., examine) themselves, it is perhaps not surprising that Ben Sira here offers no real insight regarding how or where forgiveness might be found. However, his later suggestion that forgiveness is secured by heeding the commandments and departing from injustice (35:1–3) reflects Ben Sira's assumption that much about forgiveness is to be found in the Hebrew Scriptures.

Despite this and the importance of forgiveness within the Judeo-Christian tradition,[1] there has been rather less scholarly attention than one might imagine given to forgiveness within the Hebrew Bible/Old Testament.[2] In recent years, such neglect has perhaps been encouraged by the

---

1. See, e.g., Bash, *Forgiveness*; Bash, *Forgiveness and Christian Ethics*; and Bash, *Just Forgiveness*.

2. For exceptions to the latter point, see, e.g., the contributions by McConville and Reimer cited in the bibliography of this volume.

suggestion that the Hebrew Bible amply attests divine forgiveness but knows next to nothing of forgiveness between persons in a "modern" sense (i.e., "as a voluntary change of attitude by an individual victim toward the one who has wronged her and injured her").[3] Indeed, such a suggestion does not sit uncomfortably with David Lambert's argument that a traditional understanding of repentance in the Bible (and more recently, forgiveness in Ps 51) reflects the projection of a modern preoccupation with interiority, rather than the negotiation of external and social realities indigenous to the ancient biblical text itself.[4]

In light of such developments and the modern unsettling of Ben Sira's ancient certainties regarding forgiveness, a group of scholars gathered at Trinity College Dublin to consider where and in what form, if at all, "forgiveness" might be found in the Hebrew Bible.[5] In doing so, our interest was to investigate the ways in which the Hebrew Bible itself conceptualizes forgiveness: how and in what ways does God forgive? Where, if at all, do we see forgiveness between people in the Old Testament and what does it look like? The essays contained in this volume represent most of the answers offered by those who gathered in Dublin, along with a couple of others whose work subsequently came to the attention of the editors and seemed very fitting to include.

In the first of these essays, Richard Briggs looks for forgiveness in the traditions of Exodus. In Exod 10:17, Briggs suggests that the hardness of Pharaoh's heart leads to him being abandoned rather than forgiven, while in 23:20, the forgiveness that cannot be offered by the divine messenger leading the Hebrews onward points forward to the forgiveness that will be offered by God himself in Exod 32–34. In these latter chapters, where the Hebrews' very existence is called into question following the sacrilege of the golden calf, Briggs finds very little evidence of the interiority of forgiveness displayed in Psalms. Indeed, instead of forgiveness here being about removing a punishment that in fact follows inexorably, Briggs finds that forgiveness is required to ensure that the divine presence continues with

---

3. So Morgan, "Mercy, Repentance, and Forgiveness," 138, who sees examples of interpersonal forgiveness in the stories of Joseph and his brothers and Jacob and Esau, but argues that the Hebrew Bible's witness to it is opaque, inconsistent and very much subordinated to divine forgiveness. See also Konstan, *Before Forgiveness*.

4. Lambert, *How Repentance Became Biblical*, and Lambert, "Forgiveness."

5. The gathering took place on May 11–12, 2018, in association with the Trinity Centre for Biblical Studies and thanks to the generous sponsorship of the Loyola Institute, whose contribution to the costs of publication is gratefully and warmly acknowledged.

Israel—a presence that itself confirms that forgiveness has been granted. While Briggs finds little forgiveness worthy of the name between people in Exodus or in the "liberation" of the Hebrews from Egypt, he does suggest that the picture offered by Exod 32–34 points toward the possibility of transformation and assurance of divine forgiveness.

From the narratives of the Exodus tradition, Vincenz Heereman turns our attention to the legal traditions found in Num 15:22–31 and Lev 4—texts that advise the reader how unintentional sins arising within the Israelite community may be forgiven. Noting that Num 15 is less interested than Lev 4 in differentiating precisely who sins inadvertently, or what sacrificial rituals are required to remedy them, Heereman also considers Num 15's additional interest in the problem of intentional sin that seemingly cannot be forgiven. Heereman follows Arie Toeg in seeing Num 15:22–31 as a halakhic midrash on Lev 4, which (1) normalizes its sacrificial requirements, (2) enhances its homiletic quality by using the second person (you), and (3) highlights that forgiveness is possible because of the inadvertence of the sin. In addition to defending Toeg's view against the objections of Milgrom, Heereman draws particular attention to the notable theological corollary of the Numbers passage: despite the astonishing complexity and comprehensiveness of the sacrificial system, Num 15:22–31 takes aim at priestly presumption and seeks to safeguard divine transcendence by reminding the reader that if an Israelite or immigrant sins willfully, no purification or guilt offering will secure God's forgiveness.

The question of interpersonal forgiveness comes more clearly into view in Shepherd's treatment of the famous story of David's sparing of Nabal thanks to the intervention of his wife, Abigail (1 Sam 25). Instead of dismissing Abigail's admission of guilt for failing to keep an eye on her husband as a rhetorical flourish, Shepherd suggests the possibility that it should instead be seen as a genuine confession. In doing so, he argues that Abigail cleverly diverts David from killing her husband for a serious crime (for which she can offer no evidence of his regret) by confessing her own minor misdemeanor (for which her presence before David allows her to explicitly plead forgiveness). Confirmation that it is her own lesser transgression that Abigail asks to be "lifted up" (i.e., forgiven [v. 24]) is seemingly supplied when David not only dismisses her "in peace" (i.e., without harming her) but "lifts up" her face in doing so. While modern readers might feel uncomfortable with Abigail's confession, Shepherd suggests that Abigail's presentation of herself as a penitent and "saintly sinner" might well have been intended to explain, at least in part, why she became known as a woman of "prudence."

Still in the Former Prophets, David Firth considers the theme of forgiveness in 1–2 Kings and what light it might shed on these books' famously cryptic conclusion (2 Kgs 25:27–30). Firth begins with Solomon's prayer, noting that while סלח (to forgive) occurs in only four of Solomon's petitions, repentance and sin are central to the prayer, because the petitions flow from the first occurrence of סלח in v. 30. Firth also notes that in Solomon's prayer, forgiveness cannot be assumed automatically by the Israelite or foreigner who has sinned but depends on prayer along with repentance. Drawing attention to resonances between Solomon's prayer and the story of Naaman's healing (2 Kgs 5:1–27), Firth suggests that when the Aramean goes on to secure Elisha's proleptic exoneration for accompanying his royal master to worship Rimmon, it is an apt illustration of a foreigner being forgiven. Finally, when Solomon's prayer is seen in the background of Manasseh's unhappy end, it suggests to Firth that this king is unable to obtain forgiveness (2 Kgs 24:3) for shedding innocent blood, because in desecrating the temple, he had cut himself off from the means of obtaining it.

Michael Thigpen's interest is also in notions of repentance and forgiveness in Kings, but he seeks to interpret 1 Kgs 8, 13, and 18 in light of prophets like Jeremiah and Ezekiel, where YHWH's judgments are intended to spur the people to repentance. Thigpen argues that the people's appeals and petitions in turn prompt a form of divine forgiveness but one that is promissory at best. While this promissory forgiveness anticipates the forgiveness of sin accompanying the new covenant, Thigpen insists that it is only partial and does not effect the heart change described in the Latter Prophets. Nevertheless, he suggests that God's clemency toward even wicked kings within the narrative points the people toward a hope for divine mercy and, indeed, total forgiveness beyond the punishment of exile. Thus, rather than repentance flowing from and prompting salvation in Kings, Jeremiah, and Ezekiel, Thigpen suggests that YHWH's prompting of the people toward repentance and obedience reflects the theology of grace that undergirds all of these books.

While David Reimer notes that the wisdom of Proverbs and Ecclesiastes is more interested in avoiding the rupture of interpersonal relationships than repairing them, he suggests that the latter comes to the fore in the book of Job. Understanding forgiveness as an essential element in this process of relational reconciliation, Reimer explores Job's contribution to the topic by turning first to Job 6:14–23, where Job makes clear his conviction that his friendship with his comforters has been betrayed by their response to his plight. Instead of offering comfort as friends should do, Job finds them lying, accusing, and abandoning him (chs. 13, 16, 19, 21). In light of these developments, Reimer highlights the significance of Job's willingness in the epilogue to intercede for these friends by offering sacrifices, as he had once done for his own family in the prologue. Here Job's intercession at Eliphaz's request not only suggests a rapprochement and a reconciliation of sorts between Job and his friends but also between them and God and, indeed, between God and Job himself. Indeed, God's own interest in reconciliation is suggested to Reimer by the fact that Eliphaz's request for Job's intercession comes at the divine behest. Moreover, Job's willingness to intercede after his theophany suggests that reconciliation begins with Job's rediscovery of the "fear of the Lᴏʀᴅ."

McConville takes a wider canonical perspective in considering the Hebrew Bible's witness to interpersonal forgiveness but begins by surveying the exercise of divine forgiveness through his ordering of the world and the system of reparation seen in the cultic law. Forgiveness is God's business because however much sin against others damages human relationships, it seems to be first and foremost an offence against God, which must be remedied. In turning to interpersonal forgiveness properly, McConville returns to the story of David's encounter with Nabal and Abigail, finding in it an illustration of the refusal to avenge an offense with one's own hand, in deference to the divine purpose that seems somehow to depend on this righteous renunciation.[6] McConville finds something similar in Genesis, where the forgiveness extended by Joseph to his brothers again reflects an unwillingness to repay an evil for a good that is greater than himself and is reflective of the divine intention to preserve the house of Jacob in spite of its failings. While McConville notes that neither David's story nor Joseph's foregrounds the interiority of the one who forgives, nevertheless, both protagonists' perspective on the process of reconciliation hints, for McConville, at a therapeutic notion, in which forgiveness is afforded others because it is received from God.

Finally, despite Joseph's insistence that forgiveness is God's prerogative, Anthony Bash, too, sees Joseph's overlooking of his brothers' sin against him as at least adumbrating what we might call forgiveness. Bash sees something more akin to reconciliation in David's foregoing of vengeance against

---

6. Compare here the reading offered by Shepherd in ch. 4 below.

Absalom for killing Amnon, against Shimei for cursing David, and against Mephibosheth or Ziba after Absalom's rebellion. By contrast, Abigail's presentation of provisions makes David's "forgiveness" of Nabal rather more transactional and comparable to what occurs between Moses/God and Pharaoh in Exod 10.[7] Casting his eyes forward, Bash suggests that while the Christian emphasis on interpersonal forgiveness was anticipated by developments in Judaism before the Common Era, it was also both already implied within the Hebrew Scriptures and situated within a new interpretation of it.

Can forgiveness be found in the Hebrew Bible . . . ? The essays offered here suggest that the answer very much depends on what one means by forgiveness. Certainly, there is little found in the passages explored here of the interiority that moderns often associate with forgiveness. However, what the essays collected here do find in various corners of the Hebrew canon is a serious interest in the part played by someone who has been wronged in a process that allows that wrong to be remedied. In some cases, the wronged party seems to do little more than forego a right to revenge. In other cases (both divine and human), we see signs of rapprochement and fainter or fuller hints of a relationship restored. While such cases may not satisfy some modern definitions of forgiveness, so long as we are happy to recognize that this is what it looks like in the Hebrew Bible, then forgiveness is certainly to be found here. Indeed, that its expression here might differ in some way from modern conceptions should hardly be surprising, given that, as the final essay suggests, notions of forgiveness in later Judaism and Christianity are clearly indebted—but not fully identical—to what may be found in the Hebrew Bible.

If such conclusions sound provisional, then well they should, for we are well aware that the exploration of forgiveness in the Hebrew Bible offered here is in no way comprehensive but can only be suggestive. What it suggests is that illumination of forgiveness—or whatever one wishes to call the wronged party's contribution to the process of righting a wrong—may be found in the legal material of the Hebrew Bible, as well as its wisdom literature, the narratives of the Torah, and the Former Prophets. Our hope is that this reconnaissance—this preliminary search for forgiveness in the Old Testament—will spur others on to revisit corners in which it has been found here but also to explore others in which it may well be found in the future.

---

7. Again, compare the other studies of this 1 Samuel passage elsewhere in this book.

2

Commitments to Absence and Presence

How Exodus Constructs Forgiveness

RICHARD S. BRIGGS

Introduction

THE STUDY OF FORGIVENESS in the Hebrew Bible ranges widely over texts and conceptualities ancient and modern. Does one bring a fully formed idea of forgiveness to the biblical text and search for evidence of its presence in ancient Israel and its written traditions? Or does one follow wherever the text leads and see how the language of forgiveness is deployed in those ancient texts and, as a result, allow the idea of forgiveness to be—to some degree—reconstructed by the textual study? Doubtless, one ideal is to allow the texts and the subsequent traditions to host a back-and-forth dialogue that will let our idea of forgiveness be refined by both the biblical texts and ongoing theological (and other) traditions. The present study makes a modest contribution to this dialogue by asking how the book of Exodus constructs forgiveness. More precisely: what contribution does the book of Exodus make to the large-scale project of articulating scriptural conceptions of forgiveness? But a little ground-clearing is first necessary in light of some potentially complex hermeneutical and conceptual issues that may stand in the way of the study of forgiveness in the Hebrew Bible.

On Constructing Forgiveness

The assumption of this study is that there are multiple forms of forgiveness, attending to different kinds and aspects of wrongdoing and the relationships within which such wrongdoing occurs. One way to put this point is to say that forgiveness is, as Anthony Bash has expressed it, a social construct.[1] In theological terms, one might prefer to say that it is a theological construct. Likewise, as per many abstract ideas, it is or can be constructed by any text: both explicitly and in terms of how texts (especially narratives) portray relational disorder and reordering. Again, with a more theological focus, one may then pursue the project of asking how the biblical texts construct forgiveness. It is in this sense that I will explore how Exodus constructs, or narrates, forgiveness.

However, to join this conversation at the present time is to find oneself in the middle of a lively discussion. One particular stimulus to reflection is the work of David Lambert in his probing book on repentance, *How Repentance Became Biblical*, which explores how the idea of repentance has been developed over time in Jewish and Christian reading of Scripture. Lambert sees clearly how texts offer material that is susceptible to multiple potential readerly constructs, and his own thesis is concerned with showing that repentance is less a straightforward aspect of the subject matter of ancient biblical texts and more a readerly lens through which those texts are read—the "penitential lens," as he calls it.[2] His book operates downstream of Krister Stendahl's famous reading of Paul, in which Stendahl argues that the inner wrestling so often attributed to the apostle was in fact the "introspective conscience of the West," back-projected (as it were) on to an apostle who was rather more internally at peace with himself than his subsequent interpreters have proved to be.[3] In similar mode, Lambert explores such practices as fasting, prayer, and confession, among others, to probe just how far the language that is used for such practices really addresses an interiority prior to or "underneath" the practice. In the case of prayer, for example, he concludes that intercessory appeal "does not appear to derive its logic as a verbal expression of internal states. It is rather a series of strategies for encapsulating material realities, for communicating distress to a

---

1. See Bash, *Forgiveness*, 4–5. This theme has emerged slowly in his work, e.g., it is not particularly evident in Bash, *Forgiveness and Christian Ethics*.

2. Lambert, *How Repentance Became Biblical*, 3.

3. Stendahl, "Apostle Paul."

deity who is deemed empowered to help."[4] Likewise, where confession of sin has so often been read as "the expression of a guilty conscience," Lambert rather explores it as "establishing certain social realities, the subjection of the erstwhile victimizer to victim, and, at the same time, allowing for their successful translation."[5] Sin is articulated, says Lambert, "as effecting material states, enmeshed in social relations, and shaped according to the needs of communication, rather than as the private murmurings of any core, inner being."[6] The result of these and other explorations is an account of the self in the world of others, in the Hebrew Bible, that attends first and foremost to social and material realities, and not (in fact, not at all) to matters of "interiority."

In a disarming postscript, Lambert pulls back to survey what he may have shown. It is not that traditional readings of repentance as having a certain "essence"—rooted in an interior reality—do not make sense. Indeed, they are "consistent and compelling." But they come at a price, which concerns the propensity to rewrite other people's experiences in terms privileged by one's own interior discourse and thus, in effect, to translate practices into terms that their proponents neither use nor readily appreciate.[7]

It becomes clear, then, that the language of how a text "constructs" forgiveness (as one element of Lambert's case, which is focused on repentance) may stand in some degree of tension with a more traditional mode of reading that posits that there is an inner essence to the notion of forgiveness (or repentance), which it is then the task of the biblical interpreter to discover. In a paper building on his book, Lambert went on to explore some biblical texts that are *prima facie* counterexamples to his thesis, most notably Ps 51, with its multiple depictions of what appears to be the psalmist's inner experience.[8] As with the examples in his book-length study of repentance, Lambert is able to show that one *can* read forgiveness language, even in Ps 51, as pertaining to the negotiation of external realities in the social world of the biblical author (or speaker). But in the spirit of his own postscript, noted above, this is not the same as showing that one *must* do so or that a fully exteriorized reading is necessarily superior to a reading

4. Lambert, *How Repentance Became Biblical*, 49.

5. Lambert, *How Repentance Became Biblical*, 67.

6. Lambert, *How Repentance Became Biblical*, 67.

7. See more fully Lambert, *How Repentance Became Biblical*, 189–91.

8. Lambert, "Forgiveness," an unpublished paper at the 2018 Dublin symposium upon which the present book is based.

that allows for internal elements. Where Lambert successfully critiques an overzealous universalizing of internal categories, this is not the same as showing that internal categories may not on occasion be the best ones at hand for a specific text or a specific interpretive construction.[9]

To summarize this hermeneutical detour: my initial statement that we may bring a notion of forgiveness to the biblical text, or wait to deduce our notion of forgiveness from the biblical text, was carefully designed to accommodate a range of options with respect to how far forgiveness is located as an interior or exterior feature of human relationships—which is to say: whether forgiveness is rooted in a person's inner being or in their public navigation of social reality. I have no wish to prejudge which is the better way of approaching the matter in general. Indeed, my own view is that Lambert offers a successful rebalancing of an approach that has probably concentrated too much on interiority (and as such, his case follows on elegantly from Stendahl's earlier one), but clearly such a rebalancing can in turn stretch too far towards denying that inner categories are important, which seems hard to know in any a priori way. The task before the interpreter of the Hebrew Bible is to proceed case by case and explore how the language of forgiveness works.

The approach taken by Lambert does, however, prove to be very illuminating with regard to the book of Exodus. In what follows, I shall indeed conclude that the book of Exodus's textual constructions of forgiveness do point towards an "exterior" significance of forgiveness. It may be that third person narratives will inevitably tend this way, while first person language—such as we have in Psalms—admits of introspection that is rightly best characterized in interior language. Clearly, one cannot settle this matter with one case study alone, and my point here is to clarify that I do not intend to do so, even with a case study that follows strongly in the direction of Lambert's own study. I shall return to these wider questions briefly in the conclusion. It is time now to turn to the more focused issue: how does the book of Exodus construct forgiveness?

Approaching the Book of Exodus

We pass with undue haste over the questions of where the text of Exodus comes from, its tradition history, and compositional logic, rather as

9. An appreciate review that offers a similar critique, with a range of examples, is Moberly, "Review of David A. Lambert."

a certain angel passed with haste over certain marked doorways; and we proceed with only the text we can carry with us: the forty chapters of the canonical book of Exodus. Exodus 32–34 in particular offers a valuable focus. It has become clear in recent work that—whatever the textual prehistory— one can read Exod 32–34 (at minimum), and arguably large sections of the whole book, with profit and coherence as a holistic narrative that draws the reader through an unfolding appreciation of divine-human interaction.[10] Even recent full-scale critical commentaries that divide the book between P and non-P, perhaps the most plausible current offering in this area, tend to make little distinction between the verses we shall be considering, all of which are classified as non-P by Dozeman, for example.[11] Needless to say, other readings, pertaining to different source-critical logic, are available.

This study of Exodus will proceed as follows. First, I will examine the relatively few places where Exodus speaks directly about forgiveness. Second, I shall suggest that readers might best conceptualize (divine) forgiveness in Exodus in terms of a commitment to continued divine presence. Third, I explore several matters this raises that invite further consideration, including questions of forgiveness as transformation and the assurance of forgiveness, along with brief reflections on the extent to which divine forgiveness spills over to inform interpersonal forgiveness in Exodus. I also reflect on the nature of the link, if any, between forgiveness and liberation as they are found in Exodus.

As already discussed, the link between understanding forgiveness in Exodus and wider conceptualizations of forgiveness in Scripture and tradition is not all one way: one cannot first exegete Exodus and only then ask how its findings are taken up, because the question of how best to understand the category of forgiveness—what counts as forgiveness and how it is constructed—is not simply a given in Exodus but is inevitably informed by subsequent Scripture and tradition. In the words of the subtitle of Gary Anderson's *Christian Doctrine and the Old Testament*, one might pursue *Theology in the Service of Biblical Exegesis*. I mention Anderson because his own work will prove directly relevant to this inquiry. The wider issue stands as one marker in the present ferment over theological *and* historical-critical interpretation, neither one of which is self-sufficient without the

10. See, e.g., Fretheim, *Exodus*; Moberly, *At the Mountain of God*; and Widmer, *Moses, God, and Dynamics*, as well as more widely his *Standing in the Breach*.

11. Dozeman, *Exodus*, esp. 48–50. Neither P nor non-P predates the exile for Dozeman.

other. I will take one and then the other focus for the sake of exposition, but they are assuredly two sides of one interpretive coin.

What Exodus Says Directly about Forgiveness

What is there about forgiveness that may be read directly off the text of Exodus? Explicit reflection is rare.

The major textual focus for forgiveness in Exodus occurs in the interactions between YHWH and Moses in chs. 32–34. On the occasion of Moses being up Mount Sinai and the people building a golden calf in his absence, YHWH's wrath appears to be set against the people (32:9) before Moses intervenes, in a series of four intercessions. Here I follow Widmer in seeing these as part of a coherent and developing narrative.[12]

32:11–13	1st intercession—"turn from your fierce wrath"
32:31–32	2nd intercession—"forgive" / or "blot me out"
33:12–13, 18	3rd intercession—"show me your ways / [and] your glory"
34:9	4th intercession—"let the LORD go with us . . . pardon [us]"

At stake in these interactions are (among other things) key questions of God's forgiveness of Israel. Moses's first intercession secures God's turning from his fierce wrath: "the LORD changed his mind about the disaster that he planned to bring on his people" (32:14). Widmer comments that this verse "is not so much about divine forgiveness of Israel's sin as it is often assumed; rather, this verse is primarily about an assurance that the Sinai generation will not be eradicated and that they have a future as God's people."[13] I shall be arguing that this distinction is not as clear as Widmer's comment suggests and that it may rather be that divine forgiveness is in part understood precisely as the circumstance of having a future as God's people.

The topic comes into clearer focus in 32:32 where Moses prays "if you will forgive their sin—, but if not, then blot me out of the book you

---

12. This list is comparable to Widmer, *Standing in the Breach*, 84–95, which in turn draws from his 2004 monograph.

13. Widmer, *Standing in the Breach*, 87.

have written." To "forgive" here is נשא with חטאת as object. The book God has written is presumably a reference to some "book of life," or in other words, Moses is asking God that his own fate, of life or death, will be with the Israelites: if they are unforgiven, then he wishes to die too. A minority report finds Moses offering himself as a substitute for the Israelites here, his death in place of theirs.[14] At this stage, however, Moses is not seeking to effect such a change in God but to avoid the possibility that he will lead the Israelites without God's assistance. This is immediately after Moses announces that he will seek forgiveness (to "make atonement," כפר) for the people's great sin (32:30).

After securing God's assurance that he will not be blotted out of the book of life and having experienced God's passing before him, Moses is drawn on in the remaining interactions to seek God's continued presence. This is in part the topic of his third intercession, asking God's presence to go with him so that people may know that he has God's favor (33:14–16). Moses's fourth intercession then draws this focus on presence towards the topic of forgiveness.

Moses prays here in response to the key verse 34:7—God's self-revelation to Moses as a Lord slow to anger and abounding in חסד and אמת. Here YHWH is portrayed as describing himself as forgiving, again using נשא with a word for sin or transgression, here with the verb in participial form followed by a series of three such words: עון ופשע וחטאה (iniquity and transgression and sin [NRSV]). In other words, the forgiveness is for all kinds of wrongdoing, even—in context—the making of golden idols.[15] Quickly (so 34:8, perhaps because he is brought suddenly towards a joyful response?), Moses enjoins YHWH to travel with them, adding, "Do pardon our עון and חטאת." This verse sees the only use of "pardon" (סלח, to forgive) in the book and, in fact, its first use in the canon.[16] It is unlikely that the reader is expected to draw precise distinctions between sin, wickedness, and/or transgression in this taking up of two of the three terms from v. 7 for what is to be forgiven. More simply, Moses's double term ("iniquity" and "sin" in the NRSV) presumably indicates his admission of the seriousness of the Israelites' offence; and likewise the divinely-offered triple term in v.

14. The minority report is reviewed, and found wanting, in Houtman, *Exodus*, 3:673 and n132; cf also, in agreement, Widmer, *Standing in the Breach*, 88.

15. Houtman, *Exodus*, 3:680.

16. The word becomes frequent in Lev 4ff and is also used in Num 14:19, 20.

7 indicates the overflowing scope of divine forgiveness that is central to the divine character.

What is significant here is that Moses links God's forgiveness with his commitment to go with the Israelites in their onward journey. Forgiveness is focused around continued divine presence, rather than the removal of punishment. For it is well known that the logic of 34:6–7 juxtaposes the divine generosity of forgiveness and, indeed, slowness to anger, with judgment upon the guilty. The guilty are "by no means" cleared, and upon them iniquity is visited, in ways that recognize the impact of one person's sin on the three or four generations of the sinner's immediate extended family unit, even while God's חסד endures to uncountable generations (since "thousandth" extends the horizon beyond any imaginable foreseeable future).

As Houtman observes with respect to 34:7: "In Exodus . . . forgiveness does not translate into cancellation of guilt. For that the committed sin is too great. It is going to be punished."[17] Articulating the matter differently, but in substantive agreement, Widmer says of 34:8–9: "There is good reason to argue that Moses, even here in his final prayer, did not primarily have Israel's forgiveness (in the sense of cancellation of sins) in mind, but rather was concerned with the renewing of the covenant relationship"[18]—hence the immediately following making of a covenant in 34:10. Here and in Num 14, says Widmer, "the granting of סליחה has to do not so much with the elimination of punishment but with the preservation of the fundamental covenant relationship."[19]

Before exploring this idea further, we should note the two other explicit mentions of forgiveness in the book. One is in Ex 23:20, where an angel (מלאך) is sent ahead of the Israelites as they are about to move on from Sinai (cf 32:34, 33:2). Such an angel is, however, conspicuous by its absence in Num 10ff,[20] where the מלאך has become a pillar of fire/cloud. The מלאך might thus be construed in Exodus more neutrally as a messenger (as, for example, in the work of Houtman).[21] The Israelites are commanded to show respect for the messenger, כי לא ישׂא לפשׁעכם—"for he will not forgive your transgression" ("forgive" again being נשׂא + a word for sin, פשׁע, in this case). An immediate second כי clause is more ambiguous: כי שׁמי בקרבו

---

17. Houtman, *Exodus*, 3:711.

18. Widmer, *Standing in the Breach*, 94.

19. Widmer, *Standing in the Breach*, 94.

20. Until Num 20:16, which appears to discern angelic presence in retrospect.

21. Houtman, *Exodus*, 3:273.

("for my name is in him"), which may be a causal phrase (*because* God's name forbids him to forgive) or concessive (*even though* God's name is in him, yet he is not authorized to forgive).[22] What God can or will forgive at the golden calf is foreshadowed here. In the sense that the מלאך is to lead them on their journey, this word about forgiveness attends to the Israelites' onward progress, in ways congruent with the account I shall offer for the issues in chs. 32–34.

The other verse worth noting is 10:17, where Pharaoh enjoins Moses and Aaron after the eighth (locust) plague to "forgive my sin just this once" (or perhaps "this one last time,"[23] again using נשא with חטאת as object). In a subtle touch, the lifting of Pharaoh's sin is linked to Moses's (presumably Moses, though identified just as "he" in 10:18) going out from Pharaoh and praying to YHWH, who duly "lifts" (וישא) the locusts and drives them into the Red Sea, the "sea at the end of the world," as Batto so helpfully parses it.[24] YHWH immediately hardens Pharaoh's heart (10:20), and so there is no release from the cycle of plague-burdens and punishments, but the way the narrative works tends towards suggesting that the lifting in view when Pharaoh pleads for forgiveness may be limited to his desperate desire to escape from this particular plague, rather than any more lasting spiritual transaction. Thus, negatively, one might still suggest that the core link between forgiveness and ongoing presence and/or transformation is in view here, in the sense that the absence of forgiveness is marked by Pharaoh's hardness of heart.

Conceptualizing Forgiveness in Exodus

This limited direct textual data seems to offer a relatively coherent picture: that forgiveness in Exodus is narrated in terms of ongoing presence. For God to forgive the Israelites is for God to continue to go with them through the wilderness and, more than that, to set God's sight on Israel as God's inheritance (as spelled out in 34:9). Moses himself may have secured his sense of God's forgiveness by the end of his third intercession and its response, where God's goodness (or glory) passes in front of him, but in light of the divine self-revelation of 34:6–7, Moses can see that one further step

---

22. The latter option is favoured by Houtman, *Exodus*, 3:275.

23. This is the gist of Houtman's reading of אך הפעם, *Exodus*, 2:112.

24. Batto, "Reed Sea."

is needed for the Israelites to know that God has forgiven them. The further step is divine presence.

Thomas Dozeman has suggested that divine presence is in some ways a governing rubric for the second half of Exodus: "The second half of the book, 15:22—40:38, describes the ways in which Yahweh is present with Israel in this world. . . . [The wilderness stories] elaborate on the different ways that Yahweh will be present with Israel and what obligations Israel must assume in order to live in the presence of God."[25] This notion of divine presence is constructed in various ways in Exodus, including in terms of the descent of the pillar of cloud over the tent of meeting in 33:9, in a passage widely treated in source-critical terms as an awkward interlude, although it is a particular focus of Moberly's account to see its present location as a deliberate and significant pointer to the fragile status of divine presence at a key moment in the unfolding narrative of ch. 33.[26] But what does it mean to say that God is present with Israel? Ultimately, this is the language of mystery, irreducible to factual assertions but indicating profound commitments both from Israel to God and in Israel's sense of how God is involved in Israel's life.[27] For our purposes, the key point is that one of the constructions of divine presence in Exodus configures divine presence as one element of forgiveness.

Most simply put: God can be present with a sinful people only if God forgives them. It is worth noting that this is articulated in ongoing terms, most clearly in 34:9—"Let the LORD go with us"—referring to a journey that remains to be undertaken. Several points deserve further consideration. I shall take up four of them in the remainder of this study.

Forgiveness and Transformation

First, by casting forgiveness in relational terms, Exodus leans towards accounts that express forgiveness in terms of transformation. Gary Anderson writes: "Forgiveness is not simply God waving his hand and magically

25. Dozeman, *Exodus*, 45, 46.

26. Moberly, *At the Mountain of God*, 63–66, cf 195 n5: "The argument that Yahweh's accompaniment of Israel in a shrine is a major concern of Ex. 32–34 will be one of the most novel features of this exegesis."

27. This is, says Moberly, a "paradox," and any such language that attempts to parse immanence and transcendence represents a problem that "cannot, as such, be resolved" (*At the Mountain of God*, 66).

erasing whatever wrongs have been committed (the so-called forensic approach). Forgiveness is, at its core, a process of *transformation*."[28] In his various works on sin and charity in the Old Testament and beyond, Anderson has suggested that this dimension of forgiveness has been obscured in biblical texts by Reformation-era polemics that sought to find ways of conceptualizing divine forgiveness as separated off from human endeavor.[29] The nexus of issues this raised in medieval times concerning moral standing, human effort, and responsiveness to divine grace cannot easily be unpicked, but Anderson suggests that there are clear scriptural foundations for Israel's understanding of works of charity as contributing to the paying down of sin.[30] The fundamental issue here concerns seeing divine initiative and human response as noncompetitive categories, which Catholic and Protestant theologies can both seek to do, albeit with key differences. In the sure and certain knowledge of oversimplifying: Protestant frameworks defer human response to a subsequent celebratory stage of sanctification after the done deal of forgiveness, while Catholic frameworks incorporate the "response" of the inner transformation of the believer into the divine initiative of forgiveness, with the result that forgiveness is worked out through various practices that help to effect it. This is the model Anderson sees as the Old Testament's later development of a financial symbolism for debt, whereby sinners may draw on the treasury of merits (of the fathers, for instance), as compared to earlier conceptualizations of sin as a burden to be lifted.[31] The lifting of a burden (the "lifting of sin," as Exodus might put it) appears at first glance to lean towards juridical categories of in or out: burdened/unburdened and unforgiven/forgiven. However, what I have suggested in this study is that the earlier conceptuality still works with a notion of ongoing transformation, because even burden-lifting is construed as relating to ongoing relationship. The burden is lifted to facilitate the onward journey, as we might say.

---

28. Anderson, *Christian Doctrine*, 206; emphasis original.

29. See Anderson, *Sin*, e.g., 160–63, and his *Charity*, e.g., his discussion on purgatory, 162–81, which is reprinted in *Christian Doctrine*, 185–203.

30. This becomes the practice of almsgiving, as explored in the wide-ranging study of Downs, *Alms*. Anderson takes him to task for not granting the weight of the OT backing for this conceptuality (*Christian Doctrine*, 205–6). The end result of both scholars' work, however, is comparable regarding the substantive significance of almsgiving to Judaeo-Christian faith.

31. Anderson, *Sin*, 15–39.

We may note also that the transformation in view is itself relational, i.e., external to the self, concerning ongoing interaction in the journey ahead, rather than being internal to the person forgiven. This is of a piece with saying that the wrongdoing in question is better understood under the rubric of shame than guilt, as well as being of a piece with noting that forgiveness is addressed to the Israelites as a whole rather than individuals. It is noteworthy, for example, that no record of Aaron personally receiving forgiveness is included, despite his lead role in the golden calf incident and then in turn his continued role as high priest. The forgiveness of Aaron seems understood as caught up in the forgiveness of Israel.

Forgiveness and Assurance

Second, by casting forgiveness in terms of presence, Exodus leans towards accounts that tie forgiveness to the experience—or perhaps the assurance— of forgiveness. This again offers an alternative conceptuality to language of whether one is forgiven or not and suggests that the question is not about a state of being forgiven but about the experience of being forgiven, which returns us to the nature of the ongoing relationship that marks forgiveness. Hence, forgiveness is assured only in the kinds of ways that any relational issue can be assured or, in other words, a little bit like Schrödinger's cat: an ongoing relationship is known to have succeeded in being ongoing only on the final day, when the box is opened and the cat is alive or dead—or when the book of life is opened and one's name is or is not blotted out.

In the meantime, may one have confidence that one is forgiven? Is God's forgiveness in Exodus dependable? Its dependability seems predicated entirely on the reliability of God as attested in the divine self-revelation: note the repeated emphasis on God's חסד that underlies his self-description as a God of forgiveness. This would still be true "if God did not go with Israel" (cf 34:9), but I wonder whether Moses's intercession in 34:9 is thus turned towards the question of assurance rather than actual forgiveness? In other words, Exod 32–34 indicates that forgiveness plus presence can be construed as the assurance of forgiveness, while forgiveness plus absence may well be forgiveness but will not be assured and also will not be known externally, i.e., to other witnesses. (Conceivably, this is in turn relevant to understanding the theological dynamics of the exile of the Northern Kingdom after another narration of a golden calf incident in 1 Kgs 12:25–33.) Exodus leans in the direction of underlining Moses's pressing God regarding the need for assurance and God graciously giving it. Perhaps, therefore, one may say that Exodus constructs forgiveness as something to be grasped with confidence?

Divine and Interpersonal Forgiveness

Third, the focus on forgiveness in Exodus is in terms of divine-human (specifically divine-Israel) relationships and not at all on interpersonal relationships. With forgiveness constructed as presence, in Exodus, this opens up a way of thinking about forgiveness that might explain some of the difficulties in relating it to interpersonal issues. Namely: divine presence is itself a subtle and nuanced concept, capable of a range of interpretations and patient of being construed in and through a range of experiences.[32] Human presence, however, is less conceptually complex. On one level, human presence is physical presence. There are, of course, some ramifying complexities: forms of human presence that we might describe more as emotional, psychological, carried by memory whether collective or otherwise, and so forth. But part of the difficulty of drawing any straightforward implications for the practices of human forgiveness is precisely that human physical presence is a blunt tool for representing ongoing relationship, even if it is nevertheless the most obvious tool. So while ongoing physical presence in a relationship might indeed be one powerful form of interpersonal forgiveness (i.e., remaining with a friend or loved one whom one has forgiven), it is clearly not true that this is the required human form of forgiveness always and everywhere.

The book of Exodus does not offer much help with this issue. The only narrative that touches on it in Exodus is Pharaoh's request for forgiveness from Moses and Aaron, albeit that they stand proxy for YHWH at this point, in 10:17. Egypt is simply an enemy to be abandoned: its oppression of Israel is not a relationship marred by a burden to be lifted or a debt to be paid down. Israel's Scripture will remain silent throughout on the potential for Egypt to be forgiven by Israel, and even at its most prophetically expansive will only hint at Egypt being forgiven by Israel's God (Isa 19 being the most striking example).

---

32. For an illuminating account of developing conceptions of how divine presence is encountered in the Old Testament, see Kugel, *Great Shift*.

Forgiveness and Liberation

This last observation invites one brief reflection on the absence of a category of liberation, either in my own analysis or in the book of Exodus itself. It is a well-known debate that considers the extent to which one might conceive of the exodus as liberation, with Jon Levenson arguing strongly, and in my view convincingly, that more is lost than gained by such a move, and in particular that what is lost is the Jewish specificity of YHWH's releasing of Israel from service to Egypt, which Levenson rightly insists is fundamentally about a transfer of service to YHWH himself, rather than liberation from service.[33] Interestingly, while "liberation" has often been used to articulate notions of salvation ("liberation from" pointing to "salvation from," notably in Christian liberation theologies), it is not clear how one could construe Israel's exodus as an instance of forgiveness as such. Israel is not released from slavery as an instance of forgiveness or in order to be forgiven, and as noted above, Egypt is not forgiven. Nevertheless, the conceptuality of this lack of forgiveness, as narrated in Exodus, chimes with what I have argued above: YHWH's judgment on Egypt (and/or Pharaoh) results in the removal of Egypt's presence from Israel's horizon—or more prosaically, the physical removal of Israel herself from Egypt. Lack of forgiveness as absence would exemplify the same logic as we have been exploring about forgiveness as presence. I simply note here that this is not itself a reflection on liberation, which remains an awkward category for the book of Exodus.

Conclusion

The interplay between the book of Exodus on forgiveness and later categories and questions about forgiveness brings us back to the opening discussion of how forgiveness in Jewish and Christian Scripture may best be studied. In the foregoing analysis we have seen how the book of Exodus may indeed host a dialogue between later conceptions of forgiveness and the nearer-at-hand conceptualities that are foregrounded in the text. This dialogue offers ways to tease out elements of transformation and assurance in divine forgiveness and may perhaps point to difficulties in applying these insights to interpersonal forgiveness or in relating them to liberation. These portraits of forgiveness in Exodus may therefore take their place as part of

33. See Levenson, "Exodus and Liberation." A range of interaction on this piece may be found in Bellis and Kaminsky, eds., *Jews, Christians, and Theology*.

the bigger project of constructing a scriptural picture of forgiveness, including as a Christian practice to be informed by Christianity's Old Testament.

Without prejudice to the broader discussion of inner and outer elements of forgiveness, it is certainly striking that when Exodus touches on forgiveness, it is indeed in terms of focusing on the material and social realities that are effected in forgiving and being forgiven. One is not released from slavery in Egypt in an inner sense of personal freedom. One actually leaves. Yet once again, the polarizing of interior and exterior elements is unhelpful. Since I have urged that Exodus constructs forgiveness in terms of commitments to (divine) presence or absence, the social and material realities concerned relate to what it means for God to be present or absent in one's social/material world. This is exterior to the inner self but, nevertheless, is no less mysterious, and I suggest that the ongoing intangibility of this criterion (divine presence) mitigates against thinking that exterior accounts of forgiveness are altogether separable from interior ones. Ultimately, it is the inherent complexity of achieving personal forgiveness—divine and/or human—that renders any satisfactory account of it nuanced, in the book of Exodus and beyond.

3

Sacrificial Atonement in Numbers 15:22–31

Theological Implications of an Unforgivable Sin

Vincenz Heereman

READERS AND COMMENTATORS OF the Torah have long puzzled over the lack of congruence between two passages apparently concerned with the same issue. Leviticus 4 offers a detailed series of instructions on how the Israelites are to proceed when they sin inadvertently (בשגגה).[1] The topic of unintentional offenses and their corresponding purification offerings (חטאת)[2] is picked up again in a section of Num 15, a chapter containing apparently miscellaneous cultic instructions and a brief narrative curiously wedged between the storytelling chapters dealing with the spies (chs. 13–14)

1. * The idea for this paper was suggested to me by Gary A. Anderson in the course of a wonderfully stimulating doctoral seminar on sin and forgiveness in the Old Testament. I will use שגגה (pl. שגגות) as a convenient shorthand for "inadvertent sin."

2. For the translation of חטאת as "purification offering" rather than "sin offering" (as translated in NJPS, NRSV, and most others) see Jacob Milgrom's short note "Sin-Offering or Purification-Offering?"; and see his later *Leviticus 1–16*, 253–54. He convincingly argues that several cases where this offering is required (such as the completion of a Nazirite vow [Num 6] or upon recovery from childbirth [Lev 12]) make it abundantly clear that the occasion for the offering implies no preceding sin.

and the rebellion of Korah, Dathan, and Abiram (Num 16). I will briefly rehearse the most significant divergences between the two texts and proposed solutions as to how the two texts (Lev 4 and Num 15) relate to each other. In some more detail, I examine the case that has been made by the Israeli scholar Arie Toeg, arguing that Num 15:22–31 is a halakhic midrash on the laws previously articulated in Lev 4. In reviewing some of the objections that have been raised against Toeg's proposal, it becomes apparent that his argument is still the most likely explanation for the phenomenon under discussion. Most importantly, I explore some theological questions that follow from Toeg's analysis. I argue that the author of Num 15:22–31 offers a priestly critique of the priestly theology of sacrifice and atonement, pointedly counteracting the potential temptation to manipulate the Godhead.

Differences between Lev 4 and Num 15

Even a superficial glance at both texts side by side will detect several important differences. Numbers 15:22–31 is far shorter than the corresponding section in Lev 4, and while many technical details are omitted, Num 15 also adds a short treatment on a related but fundamentally new topic—that of advertent sin (Num 15:30–31). While Lev 4 discusses four categories of inadvertent sinners (the anointed priest, the congregation, a chieftain, and an individual from among the ordinary people), Num 15 is interested only in the congregation and the individual. Leviticus 4 pauses at every purification offering to offer precise instructions for imposition of hands, place of slaughter, aspersion and pouring of blood, burning of fat, etc. Numbers 15 spares the reader such minutiae. In addition to this, as Arie Toeg has shown,[3] deeper differences in terms of both language and halakha emerge upon close examination.

In terms of halakha, the two passages differ in their range of applicability[4] as well as the animals to be sacrificed.[5] Furthermore, in Num 15:30–31,

3. See Toeg, "Numbers 15:22–31." This paper is greatly indebted to Toeg's insights. In this first section, I follow his analysis closely.

4. Leviticus 4 deals with inadvertent transgressions of prohibitive commandments (Lev 4:2, 13, 22, 27), whereas Num 15 more broadly applies to transgressions of *any* Mosaic commandment (Num 15:22). Furthermore, Num 15 stresses that the laws apply to both stranger (גר) and Israelite (אזרח), a point not made in Lev 4.

5. While Lev 4:14 has the congregation offer a bull as a purification offering, Num 15:24 requires a more complex string of sacrifices (bull as burnt offering, meal offering and libation, he-goat as purification offering). Note that the bull is a purification offering

an entirely new legal category is introduced, that of the intentional sinner or "*mezid*" (מזיד).[6] For this sinner, there is no atoning sacrifice, no forgiveness. His fate is that of *karet*.[7] This affirmation has no parallel in Lev 4 (nor in any other passage of priestly legislation). All other cases of *karet* concern specific sins, the common denominator of which, thus Toeg, seems to be "a special category of cultic sins."[8] In Num 15, this uncommonly severe punishment is extended to any sin that is committed intentionally.

Linguistically, the relatively short passage under examination (Num 15:22–31) presents a significant number of unusual features. Several expressions are syntactically rare and not to be found elsewhere in the Hebrew Bible.[9] Certain terms mentioned in Lev 4 are used in Num 15 with greater frequency. This is the case with the terms כפר pi'el (atone) and סלח nif'al (be forgiven).[10] Finally, and most notably, the terms for inadvertent

---

in Lev 4, whereas it is a burnt offering in Num 15. Usually, if a burnt offering is attached to a purification offering, it is offered after it, not before (cf. Ex 29; Lev 5:7–10; 8–9; 14:1–32; 19, Num 6:9–12). Cf. Toeg, "Numbers 15:22–31," 6n12.

6. The verb זיד (hif'il), with the meaning "to behave presumptuously" (*HALOT* 1:268), occurs in other texts of the Hebrew Bible (Neh 9:10, 16, 29; Deut 1:43; 17:13; 18:20). The participial form *mezid* (מזיד), later to become a common technical term in rabbinic literature, is first attested in the Hebrew fragment of Sir 3:16 ("Whoever forsakes a father is like a blasphemer [מזיד], and whoever angers a mother is cursed by the Lord" [NRSV]). For a typical example of usage in rabbinic context, see m. Ter. 2:3: "He who immerses vessels on the sabbath, sins inadvertently [שגג]. He who uses them, sins defiantly [מזיד]" (my translation). For the sake of convenience, I will adopt the term *mezid* (מזיד) to speak of one who sins deliberately even though it is not used in our passage.

7. I follow Milgrom, *Numbers*, 405–8, in using this term (*karet*) to describe the punishment that is reserved here for the *mezid*. The term belongs, again, properly to rabbinic vocabulary, cf. Jastrow, *Dictionary of Targumim*, 674, where the meaning "excommunication, extermination" is given. It is based on the root כרת, frequently used to indicate a specific type of punishment in the Hebrew Bible. According to Milgrom, this form of punishment, the exaction of which is reserved to God, can have two non-mutually exclusive meanings: the extirpation of the offender's line and being denied life in the world to come.

8. Toeg, "Numbers 15:22–31," 2 (translations from Toeg are mine). The instances he refers to are Gen 17:14, Ex 31:14, Lev 18:29.

9. Thus, for instance, the expression in Num 15:24 מעיני העדה נעשתה לשגגה (through the inadvertence of the community [NJPS], or without the knowledge of the congregation [NRSV, ESV]). Likewise, Num 15:26: כי לכל־העם בשגגה (for it happened to the entire people through error). Unmarked translations are taken from the NJPS. On occasion, I make use of other translations when I find them to reflect some peculiarity of the text more appropriately.

10. In Lev 4, they are used formulaically at the end of each section (Lev 4:20, 26, 31, 35). In Num 15:22–31, the terms appear in functionally equivalent formulae as well as in portions that have no counterpart in Lev 4 (cf. Num 15:26–29).

sin, שגגה and its cognate verb שגה, appearing once in each of the four sections of Lev 4, appear no fewer than nine times in the much shorter passage Num 15:22–31.[11]

Proposals Regarding the Two Texts' Mutual Relation

How then do the two passages relate to each other? The first hypothesis to be tested could be that the two passages deal with essentially the same transgressions while offering different legislation. This, of course, was unacceptable to the rabbis or, for that matter, to any reader theologically committed to the coherence of Scripture at the literal level.[12] Reflecting on the expression "if you . . . do *not* observe *all* these commandments that the LORD has spoken to Moses" (Num 15:22 ESV), some rabbinic readers have asked which sin could be so grave as to be equivalent to *not* fulfilling *all* the commandments in one fell swoop. Only idolatry, thus their answer, could be so vicious.[13] Others saw in the expression a reference to *birkat ha-Shem*, the cursing of God's holy name.[14] The rabbis' attempt at seeing Num 15 as applying only to idolatry (Lev 4 being more generally concerned with inadvertent sins of omission) cannot satisfy. As Toeg points out, the plain sense of Num 15 does not intimate such a conclusion. A transgression as grave as idolatry would certainly have been expressed explicitly.[15]

Other readers, both ancient and modern,[16] have wondered whether Lev 4 might apply to the violation of negative commandments (*mitswot lo ta'aseh* [מצות לא תעשה], in rabbinic parlance), while Num 15 would deal with that of positive commandments (*mitswot 'aseh* [מצות עשה]). This solution "was faulted by Ramban who noted that the Numbers passage cannot

11. Gane, "Loyalty and Scope," suggests that some of the peculiarities of Num 15 in comparison to Lev 4 can be explained when one resolves the issue of the apparent out-of-place character of Num 15 within the larger context of the book. For the latter difficulty, see also Novick, "Law and Loss"; Achenbach, "Complementary Reading of Torah"; and Baden, "Structure and Substance."

12. For an analysis of the same difficulty with the solution proposed by the temple scroll, see Anderson, "Interpretation of Purification Offering."

13. See b. Hor. 8a.

14. See b. Ker. 7b.

15. "As regards the opinion of the Sages, namely that the passage refers to idolatry, it is difficult to suppose that such a special case would be styled in such a generic and pale manner as we find it in Num 15: 22–23" (Toeg, "Numbers 15:22–31," 3).

16. See the references in Ashley, *Book of Numbers*, 285n4.

be limited to performative sins alone since the verb ʿasah, 'do, act,' in 'if this was done unwittingly' (v. 24), 'anyone who acts in error' (v. 29), and 'who acts defiantly' (v. 30) predicates an active violation, one that involves actually doing something rather than passively neglecting to do something."[17] It must be concluded that both passages intend the violation of *any* of the commandments. If Lev 4 narrows it down to prohibitive commandments, Num 15 deals with violations of *any* commandment *tout court*, whether *aseh* (עשה) or *lo taʿaseh* (לא תעשׂה).[18] The two passages thus partially overlap and, in doing so, partially contradict each other.

That two biblical texts could contradict each other is hardly shocking news to any modern reader. The ensuing question is: does one of the two texts build on and revise the other? In his 1903 commentary on Numbers, Gray still held that "the actual and relative antiquity of [Num 15:22–31] and Lev. 4 f. cannot be decisively determined."[19] In his opinion, "the differences are . . . due to the fact that the laws date from different periods or circles; and that the practice or theory of the one period was not that of the other."[20] Most modern exegetes, however, tend to see the two passages in a genetic relationship to one another.

---

17. Milgrom, *Numbers*, 402. For a medieval reader attentive to the plain sense of the text, see Ramban, *Commentary on the Torah*, 150. There, Ramban explains that, because of the different sacrifices commanded in Lev 4 and Num 15, the rabbis *had* to ascribe Num 15 to the sin of idolatry: "This type of sacrifice for an inadvertent sin of the congregation is different from the sacrifice mentioned in the Leviticus passage. There, one is obliged to offer a bull for the purification offering, whereas here it is a bull as a burnt offering and a he-goat as purification offering. Therefore, our rabbis *were obliged* to say that this is the sacrifice for the inadvertent sin of idolatry (*avoda zarah*)" (translation mine; emphasis added.) His own explanation of the *peshat* is that the sin in question is that of one who unwittingly becomes an apostate to the entire Torah (*mumar lekhol hatorah beshogeg*), e.g., an Israelite who grows up among gentiles unaware of his identity. Milgrom also points to *Sefer ha-Mivchar*, a Torah commentary by the Karaite exegete Aaron ben Joseph (thirteenth to fourteenth c.) who equally rejects Ibn Ezra's solution and points out that the prohibitive commandments are still called commandments. See Joseph, *Sefer ha-Mivchar ve-Tov ha-Mischar*, 407.

18. A philological difficulty militates against this proposed solution. The phraseology of Lev 4:2 (נפש כי־תחטא בשגגה מכל מצות יהוה אשר לא תעשינה ועשה מאחת מהנה) is without any ambiguity (slightly different but equally clear in vv. 13, 22, and 27). The wording of Num 15:22, however, is unusual: ולא תעשו את כל־המצות האלה. Toeg points out that no such distributive use of כל is known to him in Biblical Hebrew. The usage is, nevertheless, attested in Mishnaic Hebrew, cf. Toeg, "Numbers 15:22–31," 5.

19. G. Gray, *Critical and Exegetical Commentary*, 180.

20. G. Gray, *Critical and Exegetical Commentary*, 179.

For some scholars, Num 15 is at the origin of Lev 4.[21] The chief reason for this view lies in the assumption that, over time, traditions grow in complexity. While Num 15 knows only two categories of sin (communal or individual), Lev 4 considers four different situations (high priest, congregation, chieftain, regular individual). Num 15 only indicates the animals to be offered for each type of sacrifice, while Lev 4 specifies at some length the exact procedures to be followed in the sacrificial process. Leviticus 4 thus appears to reflect a cultic system that has grown more refined since the time Num 15 had been penned.

Yet, as Ashley points out, "it makes at least as much sense . . . to see in Num. 15 a later modification of and addition to the laws of Lev. 4–5."[22] If accrual of detail be an indicator of posteriority, Num 15 could be considered the later text on account of the multiplication and diversification of the animals to be sacrificed for public inadvertent sin in Num 15:24.

Num 15:22–31 as a Halakhic Midrash on Lev 4

The most compelling case for Num 15's dependence on Lev 4 has been made by Arie Toeg, who explains the relationship between the two by showing the former to be a halakhic midrash on the latter. Characteristic for such halakhic midrashim is the tendency to normalize halakhic prescriptions and to elaborate on preexisting material in such a way as to bring to light its undergirding theological principles.[23] In terms of halakha, the author of Num 15 faces the challenge of Lev 4 assigning a bull as the purification offering for the congregation after a שגגה—a bull, rather than the expected goat (cf. Lev 9:3; 16:15; 23:19; Num 7:28–29). He sees in the expression "a bull of the herd as a sin offering" (Lev 4:14) an abbreviated expression or, to use a Talmudic idiom, a case of *chassorei michassera* (a clause has been omitted).[24] The *darshan* fills in what is missing and reads "a bull of the herd {+ *as a burnt offering of pleasing odor to the LORD, with its proper meal offering and libation, and a he-goat +*} as a purification offering" (Num

---

21. Toeg cites Rendtorff, *Gesetze der Priesterschrift*, 14–17; Rendtorff, *Studien zur Geschichte*, 22, 83, 210; Elliott-Binns, *Book of Numbers*, 103; see Toeg, "Numbers 15:22–31," 5n10. Ashley (*Book of Numbers*, 285n5) further cites Dillmann, *Bücher Numeri*, 84, and G. Gray, *Critical and Exegetical Commentary*, 178–80.

22. Ashley, *Book of Numbers*, 285.

23. See Toeg, "Numbers 15:22–31," 7.

24. Jastrow, *Dictionary of Targumim*, 489.

15:24a).[25] The homilist thus kills two birds with one stone: he normalizes the unusual offering prescribed in Lev 4 and brings to bear the legislation concerning food offerings and libations established earlier in the chapter (Num 15:1–16). This explains why Num 15:24 has, on the one hand, the more common animal as a purification offering for the congregation, while on the other hand, against habitual practice,[26] places the burnt offering before the purification offering.[27]

Toeg finds further evidence for the homiletic character of Num 15:22–31 in its use of the second person plural to address the reader/listener. While the opening lines of both texts imply Moses's addressing the Israelites ("Speak to the Israelite people thus . . ." [Lev 4:1 and Num 15:1]), Lev 4 goes on to use nothing but the third person, as is common in legal texts. Our parallel passage in Num 15, however, changes several times into the second person. These instances are found in vv. 22–23 and 29, at the beginning and toward the end of the pericope, serving, as it were, as a rhetorical bracket. (As Toeg astutely observes, vv. 30–31 could only be in the third person, as is the case in all other laws ordering *karet*.) Numbers 15 presents both elements of the received text as well as innovations,[28] at times changing the source material and at times following it faithfully.[29]

---

25. The technical midrashic procedure that Toeg ("Numbers 15:22–31," 8–9) sees at work here is based on the distinction between *reisha* and *seipha* (i.e., the first and the last portion of a given expression). It is used in rabbinic exegesis when the beginning and the end of a statement are difficult to bring into accord with one another. In this case, the *reisha* (a bull from the herd) is given a new *seipha* (for a burnt offering), while the *seipha* (for a burnt offering) is given a new *reisha* (a he-goat). According to Toeg, this exegetical procedure is well known from the Talmud (see, e.g., b. Sukkah 3a) but can already be found in earlier texts such as the Samaritan Pentateuch.

26. See, e.g., Lev 8–9. In every sacrifice, whether in favor of Aaron or the people, the purification offering precedes the burnt offering.

27. Knohl discusses Toeg's proposal in detail and rejects it ("Sin Offering Law," 195). To his mind, "the language of the text in Numbers 15 deviates completely from the language in Leviticus 4. . . . This is no exegetic insertion but rather a revised and renewed version with only weak affinity to the original text." Whether Knohl does justice to the undeniable word-for-word correspondences is debatable. See below for my discussion of Milgrom's objections.

28. See Toeg, "Numbers 15:22–31," 12.

29. The third person wording of Lev 4:13 ("if it is the whole community of Israel that has erred") is changed into the second person in Num 15:22 ("if you unwittingly fail to observe"), whereas Lev 4:27 ("if any person from among the populace unwittingly incurs guilt") is followed without deviation in Num 15:27.

That Num 15 receives Lev 4 and comments on it can also be seen in the ninefold use of the root שגג and its synonymous cognate שגה.[30] As Toeg shows, this theme, present in Lev 4, is expanded in Num 15:22–31 into a theological commentary. Indeed, Num 15:25a quite closely follows Lev 4:20b in indicating the atoning effect of the purification offering and its result in divine forgiveness.[31] But Num 15:25b–26, beyond the source text of Lev 4:20, goes on to explain the reason why the congregation could hope to be forgiven in the first place:

> For it was an error (כי־שגגה הוא), and for their error (על־שגגתם) they have brought their offering, an offering by fire to the LORD and their sin offering before the LORD. The whole Israelite community and the stranger residing among them shall be forgiven, for it happened to the entire people through error (כי לכל־העם בשגגה).

In Toeg's view, the *darshan* responsible for Num 15:22–31 makes explicit the connection between the forgiveness obtained (סלח) and the inadvertence of the sin (שגג), a connection not highlighted in the characteristically dry and matter-of-fact wording of Lev 4.[32] This citing of a scriptural text, elaborating on some of its details, filling gaps, and offering theological justifications, could not be more characteristic of a midrash.[33]

Reception, Objections, and Responses

Unlike many other fine pieces of scholarship published in Hebrew, Toeg's article has received some of the attention it deserves. It became accessible to a broader audience thanks to Michael Fishbane who, in his landmark *Biblical Interpretation in Ancient Israel*, summarizes Toeg's argument and proposes further evidence for his conclusions. He argues that, despite the absence of a visible caesura, Num 15:22–31 cannot be considered as a

---

30. See Num 15:22, 24, 25 (x2), 26, 27, 28 (x2), 29.

31. Compare Num 15:25a ("The priest shall make expiation for the whole Israelite community and they shall be forgiven") with Lev 4:20b ("Thus the priest shall make expiation for them, and they shall be forgiven").

32. The three uses of שגגה in the cited passage are not simply pleonastic. Toeg shows that they serve to stress (a) the issue of forgiveness itself, (b) its relation to the purification offering, and (c) the validity of the law for both citizens and resident aliens. See Toeg, "Numbers 15:22–31," 13.

33. Seebass reaches a similar conclusion: "Zweifellos handelt es sich um *Gemeindebelehrung* und nicht um Ritualvorschiften wie in Lev *4f" (*Numeri 10,11—22,1*, 147; emphasis added).

continuation of the preceding section that is introduced as divine speech (Num 15:1–2a and 17–18a). The voice of Num 15:22–31 is neither that of God nor that of Moses, but rather that of the preacher. Proof thereof is the fact that both God and Moses are referred to in the third person in vv. 22b and 23b. For Fishbane, it follows from this observation that the preacher here refrains from incorporating his innovation in the received *traditum* and quite boldly sounds his own voice.[34] Astute as this analysis is, I am not convinced that the evidence can quite bear the full weight of the claim. With Milgrom, some might argue that vv. 22b–23 are "clearly an editorial interpolation, . . . added to underscore the fact that all the commandments are involved."[35] Unsure of the cogency of this counterclaim as well,[36] I am hesitant simply to fully accept Fishbane's claim, because first and third persons are often used with anything but flawless consistency. A prime example of this can be found in the vicinity of our very passage: "Speak to the Israelite people and say to them: When you enter the land that *I am giving* you to settle in, and would present an offering by fire to *the* LORD from the herd or from the flock" (Num 15:2–3a; emphasis added). Similarly, in Num 27:11, a divine speech is concluded with: "This shall be the law of procedure for the Israelites, in accordance with the LORD's command to Moses." Again, both the speaker and the addressee are mentioned in the third person, rather than the first and second, as could be expected.

Toeg's article was further, though less sympathetically, discussed by Jacob Milgrom.[37] In essence, Milgrom disagrees with Toeg's understanding of Num 15:22–31 as a halakhic midrash on Lev 4 and holds that "the attempt to find literary dependency between the two purification offering pericopes must be abandoned. There is no alternative but to assume that we are dealing with two independent traditions concerning the purification offering."[38] This magisterial dismissal of Toeg's proposal is based on two objections. First, Milgrom finds that Toeg offers no satisfying explanation

---

34. See Fishbane, *Biblical Interpretation*, 194.

35. Milgrom, *Numbers*, 402.

36. Stylistically and syntactically, the relative clause that begins in v. 22b is perfectly unproblematic. See, for instance, Ex 19:7 (וישם לפניהם את כל־הדברים האלה אשר צוהו יהוה). In terms of content, Milgrom's claim that the expansion to englobe all the commandments has to come from an editorial hand, seems to be dictated by his overall negative judgment of Toeg's proposal (see below).

37. Milgrom's article ("Two Pericopes") was later inserted as an excursus in his commentary (*Numbers*, 402–5).

38. Milgrom, *Numbers*, 404.

for the omission of the other two cases of purification offering (high priest and chieftain) as well as the omission of the ewe as an alternative offering for the individual. To this objection, had he not been snatched away by an untimely death, Toeg could have answered that he had indeed provided a good reason for these omissions. If Num 15:22–31 is in fact a midrash and its concern is primarily theological, then it is of no surprise that the author would reduce the legal casuistry much as he reduced the ritual detail. What matters theologically is that inadvertent sins, whether communal or individual, can be atoned for and forgiven. As for the omission of the ewe, in a homiletic context of citation and abbreviation, nothing seems more natural than to preserve the first option (i.e., the she-goat in Lev 4:27) and omit the second (i.e., the ewe in the entirely omitted section of Lev 4:32–35a).

According to Milgrom's second objection, Num 15:22–31 consistently calls the congregation by the archaic term *edah* (עדה) instead of the more common and more contemporary *qahal* (קהל) that is used throughout most of Lev 4. To this, we might answer in Toeg's stead that the word *edah* (עדה), with 110 occurrences in the Torah, can scarcely be considered a rare word that would not come naturally to any author familiar with the tradition. Furthermore, the author of Num 15:22–31 does not conjure the term out of his hat—he takes it straight from Lev 4:13! It is safe to say then that Milgrom's two objections are not weighty enough to bring down Toeg's proposal. Regarding his own above-cited appraisal that the two texts are independent traditions, one cannot but wonder how he accounts for the structural and lexical similarities, as well as the occasional word-for-word correspondences that are anything but a *quantité négligeable*.[39]

Theological Corollary

Though not without rivals, it appears that Toeg's proposal still has much to recommend it. What, to my knowledge, even those who accept his thesis have as yet neglected to do is to tease out its remarkable theological import. This task is largely governed by the question why the author of Num

---

39. Both passages deal with the sin of the congregation first, then with that of the individual. For every case, the order is the same: sin—offering—atonement and forgiveness (see Toeg, "Numbers 15:22–31," 11). Among other correspondences, the following might be particularly noteworthy: the concern for *all* of the commandments, whether negative or unspecified (Lev 4:13, Num 15:22); the use of the peculiar expression מעיני העדה or הקהל- (Lev 4:13, Num 15:24); the formula וכפר הכהן על- (Lev 4:20, Num 15:25); and especially the word-for-word identical ואם־נפש אחת תחטא בשגגה (Lev 4:27, Num 15:27).

15:22–31 undertook to re-elaborate the material from Lev 4 in the first place. Unlike Noth, who sees the modification of the sacrificial animals for the communal שגגה as the main reason for Num 15:22–31,[40] Toeg holds that it is not until the two climactic verses at the end of the passage that the homilist's intent becomes fully visible.[41] Verses 30–31, introducing the *mezid* as a completely novel legal case, have no source text to quote from or modify. While the opening of v. 30 mirrors to some extent the preceding case of individual transgression (v. 27),[42] the remainder of the section comes straight out of the *darshan's* forge and displays a rhetorical force far surpassing that of the preceding portion. It is worth pausing briefly to give it its due.

v. 30	aα	But the <u>person</u> that would act defiantly,
	aβ	whether citizen or stranger,
	aγ	it is the LORD that he reviles!
	b	Let that <u>person</u> be cut off from among his people.
v. 31	aα	For the word of the LORD he has spurned
	aβ	and his commandments he has broken
	bα	Let that <u>person</u> be utterly cut off (הכרת תכרת)
	bβ	his guilt is on him.[43]

The passage is nicely bracketed by the word "person" (נפש) at either end. Verse 30aα introduces the subject of this new legal disposition, substituting the heretofore omnipresent בשגגה with the rare expression ביד רמה (defiantly). This novelty, in stark contrast with what precedes, elicits the reader's heightened interest. Our patience, however, is put to the test, as two

---

40. See Noth, *Vierte Buch Mose*, 103. The section dedicated to the whole of Num 15 is tellingly titled "Verschiedene Nachträge kultisch-rituellen Inhalts." For references to other commentators holding a similar view on the sequence of the two passages, see Toeg, "Numbers 15:22–31," 5n11; Ashley, *Book of Numbers*, 285n7.

41. See Toeg, "Numbers 15:22–31," 14.

42. Compare v. 27 (ואם־נפש אחת תחטא) to v. 31 (והנפש אשר־תעשה).

43. This literal translation is mine.

clauses delay the actual disclosure of the verdict. The parenthetical remark in v. 30aβ, keeping the legal reach of the disposition at the widest possible scope and maintaining the reader's attention, prepares for the heavy rhetorical blow that is dealt in v. 30aγ: "it is the LORD that he reviles!"[44] The homiletic ring of this invective is hard to miss. After this first punch, the homilist solemnly pronounces the well-known legal formula "let that person be cut off from among his people."[45] This verdict, with the second and central occurrence of the word "person" (נפש), flanked by two appearances of the divine name, clearly marks the center of the pericope, the ineluctable consequence of the premises previously established. It is followed by a theological justification in v. 31a, divided into two segments, parallel in content, structure, and meter.[46] This justification (v. 31aα, כי דבר־יהוה בזה) runs somewhat parallel to the justification above in v. 25 (כי־שגגה הוא), albeit in perfect opposition. While inadvertence warranted atonement and forgiveness there, wantonness and brazen rebellion must call for superlative punishment here.[47] Finally, the homilist erupts into a violent imprecatory exclamation. This exclamation takes its content and terminology from the formula above in v. 30b ("that person" [נפש and כרת]), turning it into a passionate and maximally dramatic cry (v. 31bα, הכרת תכרת הנפש ההוא). After this, v. 31bβ is more than an afterthought. It brings another justification for the severe decree of *karet*, synthetic but powerful: for such a sin, there can be no atonement, no purification offering could wipe away (כפר) or obtain forgiveness (סלח) for such iniquity. The sinner will have to bear its full and crushing weight.[48]

44. Note the particular emphasis on the fronted direct object of the clause (את יהוה). Note further that this syntactic sequence {[[יהוה] את] + *topic* + *action*} is nowhere else to be found.

45. Aside from our passage, the formula occurs fourteen times in the Pentateuch (Gen 17:14; Ex 12:15, 19; 31:14; Lev 7:20, 21, 25, 27; 18:29; 19:8; 22:3; Num 9:13; 19:13.20).

46. Verse 31aα comprises seven syllables, v. 31aβ six syllables, making thus for a balanced parallelism.

47. It is not uncommon to find a justification introduced by כי after a *karet*-ruling, see Gen 17:14; Num 9:13; 19:13, 20. While the latter three occurrences are unlike our passage in that they justify the *karet* by citing a concrete transgression, the generic wording of Gen 17:14 (את־בריתי הפר) strongly resembles v. 31aβ (ואת־מצותו הפר).

48. I interpret v. 31bβ in light of Num 9:13 ("That person shall be cut off from his kin, for he did not present the LORD's offering at its set time; that man shall bear his guilt [חטאו ישא]"). It has been noted (Milgrom, *Numbers*, 125, c.f. 312n47) that the expression *awonah bah*, unique to our passage, "is a hybrid term comprised of '*avono yissa*' (Lev. 7:18; 19:8) and *damav bo*, 'bloodguilt is upon him' (Lev. 20:9; Ramban)." The homilist thus once more makes creative use of preexisting legal language.

It must then be asked what sin the priestly writer of Num 15:22–31 had in mind when he declared that there could be no sacrificial atonement for it. Milgrom believes that it is the sin of blasphemy. He lists Num 15:30–31 as one of nineteen sins punished with *karet* and categorizes it as "blaspheming, that is, desecrating God's name."[49] This interpretation reads the expression את־יהוה הוא מגדף as that which constitutes the *mezid's* deliberate sin. Considering the syntax of the verse, however, I believe that it rather functions as a theological evaluation of the sin that is described in the somewhat vague verbiage "the person that would act defiantly."[50] Insulting the Lord (מגדף) is the result of a sin that the text does not seem to specify.[51] Toeg suggests that this is intentional. To his mind, the *darshan* wishes to stress that the matter of the sin is of no consequence, because all the commandments emanate from the will of the divine Lawgiver and the deliberate transgression of any of them constitutes a serious act of disobedience.[52]

While it is true that the text in vv. 30–31 does not explicitly change the field of application defined in v. 22 as "all the commandments," it seems difficult to charge our author with a religious fundamentalism of such a caliber that he would see people "cut off" for the intentional transgression of any ever-so-minute law.[53] Especially in the conspicuous absence of a plan B for atonement, it is more likely that he would see this radical case applied

49. Milgrom, *Numbers*, 406.

50. In other words, Milgrom reads as follows: "Should a person act defiantly . . . by insulting the Lord, let him be cut off." Instead, I propose to read (see above): "Should a person act defiantly . . . , it is the Lord that he reviles! Let him be cut off." Note that this expression at the head of v. 30 והנפש אשר־תעשה ביד רמה parallels the beginning of v. 27 ואם־נפש אחת תחטא בשגגה where the imperfect is also used to describe a hypothetical situation. The participial construction את־יהוה הוא מגדף (v. 30aγ) seems more apt to function as a comment to that hypothetical sin expressed earlier.

51. In fact, not even the verb "to sin" is used (as in v. 27). The text is as generic as can be: "the person that would act [תעשה]."

52. Toeg compares Num 15:30–31 to the many instances in Lev 19 where all kinds of laws of seemingly varying degrees of importance are elevated to the same rank by the unvarying appendix "I am the Lord your God" (Toeg, "Numbers 15:22–31," 18). Fishbane interprets similarly, seeing as a novelty of Num 15:30–31 that any act of disobedience would call for *karet* (cf. *Biblical Interpretation*, 194).

53. Artus speaks of a radicalization intervening between the legislation of Lev 4 and that of Num 15 (Artus, *Études sur le livre*, 269). Gane points to the fact that between inadvertent sins and deliberate "high-handed" sins there is a gap, i.e., deliberate sins that are not defiant, that is simply not addressed in this pericope. Other passages clearly consider the possibility of atonement for such cases (guilt-offering in Lev 5:1, 5–6, 20–26). See Gane, *Cult and Character*, 210–13, and Gane, "Numbers 15:22–31," 154–55, both cited in Gane, "Loyalty and Scope," 253.

only in rare instances. The qualification ביד רמה should be what determines this worst of all categories of sins.[54] A sin committed as intentional insubordination and defying God's sovereignty should be closer to what the author of Num 15:22–31 probably envisaged. This assessment does not remediate the tantalizing vagueness of the text and probably with good reason. By our writer's standards, what counts is not so much the matter of the sin as its form. Any one of the commandments, great or small (and who is to say which is which?), could be broken with the intent to rebel against God and out of contempt for his word—"because he has spurned the word of the Lord" (v. 31). The gravity of the sin lies, as it were, in the sinner's internal forum. It could be a public scandal, just as it could happen in the secrecy of a tent. Insofar as it could escape human notice, it is fitting that the exaction of the penalty should be God's own responsibility.[55]

If Toeg is correct and this last section contains the chief theological message of the pericope, its daring novelty cannot be overstated. Not only does the author introduce a new legal category—the *mezid* or brazen sinner—he above all traces a boundary to one of the most far-reaching, seemingly all-embracing religious realities of ancient Israel: the priestly sacrificial system. Reading through the lengthy sections of the Pentateuch that prescribe and describe a plethora of sacrifices and offerings, one gains the impression that nothing is left out, that no event in the life of a human person is free from the cultic strings that attach it to the life of the temple. The system knows of a variety of sacrifices, each of them corresponding to a specific need. The sacrifice in the author's crosshairs here is the חטאת (purification offering). As Jacob Milgrom has convincingly shown, the primary function of this sacrifice is to decontaminate the sanctuary from impurity. This contamination arises from various circumstances, each polluting the sanctuary to a different degree and requiring a corresponding חטאת.[56] The

54. The expression ביד רמה is found elsewhere only in Ex 14:8 and Num 33:3. Labuschagne shows that in the Exodus-related passages it has distinct military overtones, with Israel as its subject defying Pharaoh and ready for battle ("Meaning of *b^eyād rāmāa*"). According to Kellermann, such a posture belongs primarily to God ("Bemerkungen zum Sündopfergesetz," 111–12). If that is correct, Achenbach argues, applying this expression to a deliberate sin by a human serves to highlight the blasphemous character of the deed ("Complementary Reading of Torah," 223–24). For a recent study arguing that ביד רמה relates to Israel's refusal to take the land and its connection to the Lord's rest, see Noonan, "High-Handed Sin."

55. Cf n7.

56. A שגגה committed by a regular individual or some case of regular physical impurity both necessitate the purification of the courtyard altar. A שגגה committed by the

text of Num 15:30–31 knows of no offering that could remediate the defilement caused by a *mezid*. In Milgrom's view, however, "sacrificial atonement is barred to the *unrepentant* sinner, to the one who 'acts defiantly (*byd rmh* . . .), reviles (*mgdp*) the Lord . . . ' (Num., xv, 30), but not to the deliberate sinner who has mitigated his offense by this repentance."[57] In fact, once the sinner has repented, his willful sin can be atoned for on the Day of Atonement when the high priest will enter into the adytum on behalf of the sinner that defiled it.[58] In this, Milgrom follows traditional rabbinic doctrine that sees the rituals of Lev 16 as atoning for the sin referred to in Num 15.[59]

With this, however, we lose sight of the finest point that follows from Toeg's analysis. However one may try to reconcile and read synchronically the different theologies of sin and atonement, the author of Num 15:22–31 clearly affirms: there are sins that *cannot* be atoned for! No purification offering and no guilt offering can wipe away such offenses. The sacrificial system by which the priests of the temple maintain, serve, and appease the presence of the deity—that system of forbidding complexity and infallible efficacy is at its wit's end when it encounters certain sins. The homilist, it seems, wants to put his fellow priests on guard against the misconception that there is a fix for every bug, a cultic trick that can remediate any mishap. By placing certain sins beyond the range of any offering's atoning efficiency, our author indirectly reminds cultic ministers of the limited character of their powers.

This insight can be corroborated by a brief glance at the usage in v. 30 of the root גדף (*piʿel*). Its meaning can be rendered as "revile, insult, taunt" and it is not frequently used in the Hebrew Bible.[60] Toeg points out that the only other passage where the verb is used to designate an offense aimed directly at God is found in Ezek 20:27.[61] There, it qualifies the sin of cultic

---

high priest or the whole community calls for a purification of the inner altar and the veil. Finally, the brazen sin committed by a *mezid* pollutes the very throne of God in the holy of holies. See Milgrom, "Israel's Sanctuary," 393.

57. Milgrom, "Priestly Doctrine of Repentance," 196; emphasis original.

58. See Milgrom, "Israel's Sanctuary," 393.

59. For further insight and sources, see Milgrom, "Priestly Doctrine of Repentance," 196n37.

60. It is used in the context of the Assyrian messengers who taunt Hezekiah and thereby, indirectly, his God. See 2 Kgs 19:6.22 // Isa 37:6.23. Further usages applied to the reviling of humans are found in Ps 44:17, as well as (in cognate forms) in Ezek 5:15, Isa 43:23, 51:7, Zeph 2:8.

61. Cf. Toeg, "Numbers 15:22–31," 18. In the passage concerning Hezekiah and the Assyrian envoys (2 Kings 19 // Isa 37), God is reviled only indirectly.

infidelity. Israel's worship of foreign gods on the high hills of the country is registered by God as an insult (גדף) and a treachery: "In this also your fathers insulted me, by dealing treacherously with me" (Ezek 20:27b, ESV, slightly modified).[62] This point of contact with the prophetic literature is perhaps not insignificant. The priestly homilist at work in Num 15 may have a kindred spirit in the priestly prophet Ezekiel. It is worth noting that in Ezekiel's understanding of history as well, Israel's sins were well beyond the atoning capacity of any sacrifice offered in the temple.[63] Both our priestly *darshan* and Ezekiel attribute great importance to the cultic dimension in the worship of Israel's God. But both seem to imply that there is a limit to what it can do. Their theology wants to provide a safeguard for divine transcendence. God's majesty is such that certain offenses cannot be expunged by human agency, no matter how well oiled the priestly sacrificial machine might appear to some of their confreres.

Our author's warning is equally intended for the potential *mezid*, i.e., any Israelite and even any resident stranger. If you are thinking about committing an intentional sin . . .—be warned, the *darshan* says, we shall not be able to do anything for you! God's holiness will be offended in a way none of our sacrifices can make amends for. Under certain circumstances, our offerings can settle your accounts with God, but do not dare to presume on God's forgiveness, the more brazenly to sin. Finally, expanding for a moment the scope of our reflection, we will find that our text has a helpful complement in what Jewish tradition has called the Thirteen Attributes of Mercy revealed in Ex 34:6–7.[64] One of them similarly points toward a concept of divine justice that does not allow sin to go unpunished: he "will by no means clear the guilty, visiting the iniquity of the fathers on the children and the children's children." While bound by his own righteous nature (what the rabbis called *midat haddin*) to restore balance on the scales of justice by prosecuting iniquity, God's innermost leaning is nevertheless toward mercy and forgiveness (*midat harachamim*). While he visits iniquity "to the third and fourth generation," he "keeps steadfast love for thousands." The stern warning implied by Num 15:22–31 helps to understand the gratuitousness

---

62. Note that here as well it is a certain sin that is qualified as insulting to God. This lends further weight to my point above in n47.

63. For a suggestive overview of Ezekiel's theology of sin and restoration, see Schwartz, "Ezekiel's Dim View." Israel's purification from her many brazen sins of infidelity comes about solely by God's decision, with neither change of heart nor sacrifices to merit such a restoration.

64. The *locus classicus* for the rabbinic discussion of this is b. Rosh Hash. 17b.

of such steadfast love and bountiful forgiveness. Israel's priests should firmly stand by this revealed truth, but they should not be so foolish as to believe themselves intimately acquainted with the secret ways of God's mercy.

4

"The Trespass of Your Servant"

Looking for Forgiveness in the Story of David, Abigail, and Nabal[1]

DAVID J. SHEPHERD

O! let my Tears and Penitence attone
For the sad ill I have so rashly done.
Pity the Sorrows of a sinful Breast,
Loaded with Grief too great to be exprest.[2]

GIVEN HOW LITTLE INTERPERSONAL forgiveness has been detected in the
Hebrew Bible, the appearance of an example in the stories about David in
1 Samuel is, in some ways, rather unexpected.[3] Indeed, given David's usual

1. While the author is, of course, solely responsible for whatever missteps remain, he
is grateful for the feedback received in Dublin, which undoubtedly placed the following
on a firmer footing.

2. Ward, *Forgiving Husband*, 4. We will see that some wish to dismiss Abigail's request
for forgiveness as nothing more than a rhetorical flourish, but the plea of Ward's Wife to
her Husband suggests that in eighteenth-century England, at least, the two need not be
mutually exclusive.

3. For useful discussions of interpersonal forgiveness in the Old Testament, see Reimer, "Stories of Forgiveness," who offers an enlightening comparison of 1 Sam 25 with

39

modus operandi,[4] one might be forgiven for wondering whether 1 Sam 25 really does contain any forgiveness after all. Because of this, or perhaps in spite of it, in the following, we wish to consider who, if anyone, appears to be forgiven in the story of David, Nabal, and Abigail, and of what?

David and Nabal: Finding Fault

Following David's sparing of Saul (though not his cloak) in the cave at En Gedi (1 Sam 24), David and his band of men are still left very much in the wilderness, which is indeed where the reader finds them as the following chapter begins ("wilderness of Paran" [25:1]).[5] From here, the narrative wastes little time in introducing and characterizing the previously unknown couple of Nabal—who is rich and irascible—and Abigail—who is discerning and beautiful (vv. 2–3).[6] It is to Nabal that David sends messengers with an apparently unsolicited report of his lack of interference with (and possible "protection" of) Nabal's sheep-shearing activities in the Carmel, for which David then appears to request favorable treatment from Nabal and material compensation.[7] Given these circumstances, it is not surprising that questions have been raised by scholars about the legitimacy

---

the stories of Joseph and his brothers and Jacob and Esau, and also Gowan, *Bible on Forgiveness*, 3–90, who sees David's forgiveness of Abigail as very much the exception to the rule insofar as the David narratives are concerned.

4. Reimer notes that the dispatching of Shimei by Solomon at David's request proves that David's earlier sparing of Shimei does not constitute forgiveness ("Stories of Forgiveness," 375). Reimer is not certain whether David forgives Saul (text unspecified, but perhaps with 1 Sam 24 and/or 26 in mind) or Absalom ("Stories of Forgiveness," 362–63), while Gowan rightly refuses to find forgiveness in David's dispensation to Absalom to return to court (2 Sam 14:33; *Bible on Forgiveness*, 89).

5. David is also bereft of any guidance from the prophet Samuel (so, e.g., Miscall, *1 Samuel*, 149), who the text notes here has died—though, as Miscall admits, this may be of little significance given that Samuel has not been of any real use to David since 1 Sam 19. Perhaps more significant is that notice of Samuel's death arrives after Saul has acknowledged to David the eventual transfer of the kingship announced earlier by Samuel to Saul (so Auld, *I & II Samuel*, 293). With this acknowledgment, Samuel rests in peace, until disturbed by the medium of Endor in 1 Sam 28.

6. If signs of multiple sources (see, e.g., Veijola, *Ewige Dynastie*, 47–80) are most clear in Abigail's plea to David, even here they have been combined with extraordinary skill and subtlety.

7. Some commentators see David as well within his rights to make the request (so Caquot and Robert, who reference later Arab customs, the relevance of which is, however, very debatable [*Livres de Samuel*, 307]).

of David's request and general behavior here.[8] The narrative itself will not be fully drawn on the question of the legitimacy of David's request nor indeed Nabal's rebuffing of it,[9] but David's immediate call to arms (25:13) and the servant's request for the urgent intervention of Nabal's wife Abigail (25:14–17) suggest that whatever the legitimacy of the request, the tenor of Nabal's reply has been seriously ill judged and has potentially put at risk the lives of Nabal and his house. That the servant's anxieties are themselves judged to be legitimate by Abigail, at least, is suggested by the urgency with which she sets out to deliver to David a collection of foodstuffs that offers both a prudent response to David's request but also a preemptive peace offering.[10] The practical necessity of this action is confirmed by the narrator's report of the view David has taken of the situation:

> 21 Now David had said, "Surely in vain have I guarded all that this fellow has in the wilderness, so that nothing was missed of all that belonged to him, and he has returned me evil for good (רעה תחת טובה). 22 God do so to the enemies of David and more also, if by morning I leave so much as one male of all who belong to him." (1 Sam 25:21–22)

While questions may remain regarding precisely how and why David's protection of Nabal's sheep shearing is "good" (v. 21), David's characterization of it as such here affirms Nabal's servant's own assessment (v. 17, "very good"). That David is presented here as contrasting his own good behavior with what he perceives to be Nabal's bad/evil behavior (v. 21) is not unexpected by the reader, who is invited to recall—and to assume that David does too—Saul's own admission to David in the previous chapter: "You are more righteous than I, for you have repaid me good (הטובה), whereas I have repaid you evil (הרעה)." (1 Sam 24:18).[11] If both Nabal's and Saul's repaying

---

8. Stoebe sees in David and his men a band of outlaws, extorting provisions in exchange for "protection" (*Erste Buch Samuelis*, 455–56); Gunn suggests a "protection racket" (*Fate of King Saul*, 97–98); and others see here something comparably untoward (e.g., Biddle, "Ancestral Motifs," 637).

9. Rosenberg leans toward seeing this as a reasonable protest against early Davidic taxation (*King and Kin*, 150), while Gordon sees Nabal's response as technically in the right given that we have no indication that David's protection was solicited (*1 & 2 Samuel*, 183).

10. Shields, "Feast Fit for a King," 47.

11. As observed by Fokkelman (*Crossing Fates*, 495), amongst others. The case for Nabal here approximating Saul in various ways has been made convincingly and at length initially by Levenson, "1 Samuel 25," 13–20; Gordon, "David's Rise," 43–51; and

of evil to David for the good he does them encourages the reader to see them as similar, the fact that David spares both of them only enhances the parallel.[12] However, while the reader is invited to acquiesce to David's sense of being badly treated by Nabal here, the servant's characterization of what David has planned for Nabal as bad/evil (הרעה 25:17;) suggests the possibility that David's call to arms and vow may not be merely different from his restraint toward Saul but in some way evil/bad itself.[13] Indeed, that David's vow is unwise may be hinted at by the similarity of his form of words here ("May God do so" [v. 22]) to those of Saul in 1 Sam 14, where Saul's own self-imprecation in swearing violence against his son (14:44) is seemingly preempted by the people's own deliverance of Saul. Saul's imprecation of himself there and Abner's similar vow in abandoning Ish-bosheth in 2 Sam 3:9 have persuaded some that David's vow here originally read or should be read as a conditional self-imprecation (i.e., "May God do so to me") rather than a cursing of David's enemies, as the Hebrew in its current form suggests. However, if the current form of David's vow might encourage the reader to expect David to go on to curse himself, Abigail's mention of David's enemies later in this chapter, and the preceding chapters' interest in David's enemies, strengthen the case that David is cursing them, too, here, rather than himself.

Earlier in 1 Samuel, Saul's wish to be avenged on his enemies (including and perhaps preeminently, David [18:25]) and the narrator's underlining of Saul's perception of David as his enemy (18:29; cf. also 19:7) gives way to the characterization of Saul as David's enemy in ch. 20. There, Jonathan first imprecates himself (v. 13) in case he fails to inform David of Saul's intentions and then prays that the LORD will cut off the "enemies of David, every one from the face of the earth" (20:15; cf. also v. 16).[14] This reversal is completed in ch. 24, where, as we have seen, Saul is the very "enemy" that David's men insist has been divinely delivered into David's hands (24:5), and Saul invokes the LORD's reward (v. 19) for David for sparing him on the grounds that "if a man finds his enemy, will he let him go away safe?"[15]

---

regularly by others since (for literature and useful comments, see Green, *How Are Mighty Fallen*, 392). Nicol, "David, Abigail," 135–36, remains unconvinced.

12. So Gordon, *1 & 2 Samuel*, 184, and Polzin, *Samuel and the Deuteronomist*, 211.

13. This complicates the suggestion of Chapman that the narrative here wishes to endorse unreservedly David's intended course of action against Nabal (*1 Samuel*, 190).

14. 1 Samuel 20:16 is unclear in the Hebrew but invokes the Lord and mentions David's enemies.

15. Polzin notes that Saul wishes God to reward David for doing what he himself did

While the emphasis on David's scrupulous restraint toward Saul in 1 Sam 24 makes the lack of it in relation to Nabal here rather unexpected, it seems clear that the characterization of Saul as David's enemy in the preceding chapters serves to sharpen this contrast and to make David's cursing of his enemies here (rather than his sparing of them or even doing good to them) all the more shocking.[16] Indeed, rather than the Lord being invoked to reward David for not slaying his enemy, or to eliminate David's enemies on his behalf, the Lord is invoked here by David to complete the destruction of David's enemies (including but perhaps not limited to Nabal), which will be begun by David's own hand.

The servant's concern that David intends to bring about not only the end of Nabal, but "all his house" (כל־ביתו [v. 17]) is seemingly confirmed by David's vow to not leave alive "one who urinates against a wall" (משתין בקיר [v. 22])—a phrase that may reflect David's pejoration and/or his passion but seems more probably to describe not merely a male but one who might have hope of producing progeny.[17]

In view of the preceding narrative, David's intention to destroy Nabal's house (now and hereafter), with the Lord's assistance, if necessary, might be seen to offer unexpected validation of Jonathan's (20:15) and Saul's efforts (24:21) to extract vows from David that he will not destroy their "houses."[18] David's vow against Nabal's house does not necessarily imply that he will not keep his vows to Jonathan and Saul, but the targeting of not merely Nabal but also his house demonstrates to the reader not only the depth of the insult to David but also a side of David that has not been glimpsed before: while Saul had sought to annihilate Ahimelech and his house for the

---

with Agag (i.e., the sparing a royal enemy [1 Sam 15]; *1 Samuel*, 190). That Saul paid for doing so with the loss of his kingdom makes his endorsement of his own kingdom as David's reward for sparing him more than a little ironic, especially given that Saul cannot seem to resist seeking David's life.

16. It is very likely therefore, at least as original as Abigail's own invocation of the Lord against David's enemies later in this chapter. If David's enemies have been added to what was originally a self-imprecation, then this may well have been in conjunction with the insertion of ch. 25 between 24 and 26.

17. This seems preferable in light of the appearance of this phrase elsewhere, where the elimination of a dynasty or "house" is also in view: 1 Kgs 14:10; 16:11; 21:21; 2 Kgs 9:8. For this proposal and a review of previous ones, see D. Smith, "Pisser against a Wall." In view of this evidence, and the text's general thrust, the suggestion of Miscall, that David is presented as never really intending to kill Nabal (*1 Samuel*, 155), may be set aside as distinctly improbable.

18. So Leithart, "Nabal and His Wine," 526.

betrayal of providing provisions for David and his men (1 Sam 21–22), here David seeks to annihilate Nabal and his house for the betrayal of failing to provide provisions.[19]

David and Abigail: Finding Forgiveness

If the reader is thus left in little doubt regarding David's intention to destroy Nabal, the verses that follow (vv. 23–31) document with equal clarity the lengths to which Abigail goes to divert him.

> 23 When Abigail saw David, she hurried and got down from the donkey and fell before David on her face and bowed to the ground. 24 She fell at his feet and said, "On me alone, my lord, be the guilt. Please let your servant speak in your ears, and hear the words of your servant. 25 Let not my lord regard this worthless fellow, Nabal, for as his name is, so is he. Nabal is his name, and folly is with him. But I your [maid-]servant did not see the young men of my lord, whom you sent." (1 Sam 25:23–25 ESV)

Abigail's urgency (v. 23) and the narrative's emphasis on her obeisance (vv. 23, 24)[20] prepare David and the reader for an appeal that begins with the entreaty found in v. 24. On the face of it, Abigail's words here (בי־אני אדני העון [literally, in or on me, me, my lord, is the guilt]) very much give the impression of someone assuming responsibility for what has happened. Yet Abigail goes on in v. 25 to seemingly admit what the reader knows already—that the offense against David has arisen because of her reckless fool of a husband rather than Abigail's own failing.[21] That Abigail is offering more of a rhetorical flourish here than a real admission of guilt seems even more likely to some, in light of the similarity of her words to those spoken by another woman who seeks to persuade David to do something in 2 Sam 14. There, the woman of Tekoa asks David to save her fictional fratricide son but recognizes that, in asking David to prevent the exercise of blood vengeance, she is asking the king to leave his house vulnerable

---

19. Polzin, *Samuel and the Deuteronomist*, 211.

20. While it is possible that the repetition of Abigail's falling at David's feet (lacking in LXX but present in MT) is evidence of multiple sources, it is not impossible that the text means to refer to repeated prostration (so H. Smith, *Books of Samuel*, 227), which would certainly emphasize Abigail's obeisance.

21. Leading some to misunderstand Abigail as apologizing for "her speech" (so Bridge, "Desperation to a Desperado").

to bloodguilt. Seeing that David's initial response to her is ambiguous, the woman of Tekoa seeks to fully persuade King David to intervene by insisting that עלי אדני המלך העון (upon me, my lord, the king, be the guilt [14:19]). Various commentators, judging that the Tekoite woman's offer cannot be taken seriously, conclude that Abigail's own insistence on her guilt here cannot either. For example, Caquot and Robert see Abigail's assumption of blame as nothing more than, as they put it, "the customary self-deprecation of a woman before a man" (noting 2 Sam 14:19).[22] McCarter and Jobling are similarly content to relegate Abigail's apparent owning of the guilt here to the category of "opening courtesies,"[23] while Campbell suggests that Abigail's assumption of guilt merely ensures that her plea receives a hearing.[24] Fokkelman, for his part, favors interpreting Abigail as expressing merely a wish, rather than a statement of fact, which he suspects may well be true of the Tekoite as well.[25] But, as Fokkelman himself admits, this makes little difference in 1 Sam 25, given that in his view, Abigail goes on to make it clear that the real fault to be forgiven belongs to her husband.[26] In comparing the pleas of the two women, however, it is worth noting that whereas the Tekoite woman offers the reader no further reason to take *her* wish to claim the guilt seriously, the same cannot be said for Abigail, who goes on to supply both David and the reader with precisely this. While it is true that Abigail does, in v. 25, indict her husband's foolishness, or worse, her point is not merely to excuse him but to incriminate herself: ואני אמתך לא ראיתי את־נערי אדני (But I your servant did not see the young men of my lord, whom you sent).[27]

---

22. Caquot and Robert, *Livres de Samuel*, 310.

23. While McCarter is right to suggest that the guilt that Abigail claims is neither Nabal's nor the bloodguilt of which she will warn David (*I Samuel*, 398), McCarter's insistence that Abigail here merely owns whatever blame might arise from the following conversation fails to account for the specific guilt to which both Abigail and the woman of Tekoa (2 Sam 24) will specifically refer. Indeed, even if McCarter's suggestion were plausible, it is difficult to see how it would not amount to rather more than "simply a part of the conventions of courteous and respectful behavior" that he (and others who have followed him) claim it to be. See also Jobling, *1 Samuel*, 153.

24. Campbell, *1 Samuel*, 260.

25. See also Klein, who contemplates whether Abigail is offering to bear the blame for Nabal (*1 Samuel*, 250) but ultimately seems to follow McCarter.

26. Fokkelman, *Crossing Fates*, 398–99. Firth simply observes that Abigail's humbling of herself before David gives rhetorical force to her claim to bear Nabal's guilt (*1 Samuel*, 251).

27. Hertzberg acknowledges that "she takes the guilt for everything upon herself, for

As others have noted, Abigail's reference to herself as "your servant" and David as "my lord" underlines her deference,[28] but perhaps even more crucial is her fronting of the independent pronoun "I" (אנכי), which allows her to connect the guilt that she has just admitted with her failure to intervene outlined here. While Abigail's "not seeing" might seem a small failing in comparison with Nabal's offense, taking Abigail at her word in fact allows us to understand her earlier claim to guilt more clearly.[29] In v. 24, Abigail simply insists or wishes for David to consider her failing the relevant one, as if to say: "in me or upon me be the guilt that is relevant." There are, of course, various reasons why she might wish for David to focus on her guilt instead of Nabal's. On one hand, as some have pointed out, it is possible that Abigail's status as a woman might have offered her a protection from David that her husband as a man might not have enjoyed.[30] Indeed, the narrator's report of David's intention to dispatch only the "males" of Nabal's house (v. 22) might suggest as much, though this requires Abigail to both know of this or assume it and to understand it as qualifying the servant's report to her that David intends evil for Nabal and "all his house" (v. 17). Such a possibility also requires that the "hurt/evil" David later claims he would have done to Abigail (v. 34) be understood as quite different in kind from his intended massacre of Nabal's men and perhaps merely a byproduct of it. Alternatively or additionally, Abigail may prefer to confess her "sin" because it is less egregious than her husband's and thus easier for David to forgive. Indeed, the fact that most commentators dismiss Abigail's claimed offense entirely rather proves this point.[31] Perhaps most importantly, it should be noted that it is Abigail's assertion—that her failure rather than her husband's is the relevant one—that allows her to plead for forgiveness for herself, rather than for Nabal, whose own contrition Abigail cannot easily

---

she—as she says later—did not see the messengers" (*I & II Samuel*, 203). Auld agrees that she takes the guilt on herself, admitting "her own responsibility for what she has not done" (*I & II Samuel*, 299). See also Steinmann, *1 Samuel*, 486.

28. E.g., Firth, *1 & 2 Samuel*, 270.

29. Contra I. Fischer, who acknowledges that Abigail assumes the blame/guilt, but claims that the text does not make clear for what ("Abigajil," 54).

30. So Esler, "Abigail," 177; Baldwin, *1 and 2 Samuel*, 161; and Tsumura, *First Book of Samuel*, 588.

31. If it is objected that a wife is not required by law to keep an eye on her husband and save him from his own foolishness, it might be pointed out that neither does it require Nabal to pay David for protection, which may well fall into the category of a customary obligation.

prove in her husband's absence. Indeed, her further double exhortation to David in v. 24 to listen to the words of "your maidservant" highlights that David should attend to the words of Abigail, who is, at least, present, unlike her husband, of whose remorse David has no evidence.[32] Thus, instead of pleading for forgiveness for an egregious crime committed by her husband, who is not (and perhaps cannot be) shown to be sorry, it seems more likely that Abigail here pleads instead for forgiveness for a mere misdemeanor committed by herself, for which she will present herself as being very sorry indeed, as we shall soon see.[33]

But before she makes this clear, Abigail in v. 26 turns her attention to why David must not, and indeed need not, raise his hand against her husband, expressing her wish that David's enemies and those who seek David's life (vv. 26, 29) will be like Nabal.[34] More precisely, her wish is that they, like Nabal, will not be killed by David himself, as demonstrated by the premising of this wish on her claim in v. 26 that the Lord has restrained David from bloodguilt, literally "going into bloods" (מבוא בדמים) and from saving with his own hand.[35] That it is the sparing of David, rather than the sparing of Nabal, that is Abigail's primary concern is hinted at here by Abigail and will be made still clearer in a moment. Before doing so, however, Abigail presses David in v. 27 to accept "the blessing" (הברכה) of food provisions that Nabal understood David to be asking for in the first place (v. 11) and denied him. But in view of Abigail's claim that she is in fact at fault, her belated offering of the foodstuffs must be seen not merely as an attempt to mitigate her husband's sin of commission but also her own sin of omission, in failing to observe the arrival of David's men.

---

32. By way of general observation, this suggests that for the writer of 1 Sam 25, at least, confession and contrition may be integral to the process of forgiveness, whether this is the case in other narratives or not.

33. Thus, we suggest something slightly different from others who also take seriously Abigail's profession of guilt. See, for instance, Levenson, who suggests that Abigail "disarms David by taking full blame for Nabal's irresponsibility" ("1 Samuel 25," 19); and Green who sees Abigail as requesting that David "transfer" the guilt of the refusal to her (*How Are Mighty Fallen*, 402). Cf. also Tsumura, *First Book of Samuel*, 588.

34. As Polzin notes, the fact that Nabal has in no way sought David's life as Saul has repeatedly, suggests that the reader is invited to keep the latter in mind, and strengthens the connection between ch. 25 and those that precede and follow it (*Samuel and the Deuteronomist*, 211).

35. Auld observes that while this particular expression is unique, דמים used in this way is not (*I & II Samuel*, 299). For a reading of the David stories that sees this as one of their most important concerns, see Shepherd, *King David*.

Having referred to herself as David's "maidservant" in admitting this oversight (v. 24) and having noted that the foodstuffs that would have arrived had she been watching, have now arrived by the hands of "your maidservant" (v. 27), Abigail finally makes explicit what she is asking David to do in relation to her lesser offense, namely: שָׂא נָא לְפֶשַׁע אֲמָתֶךָ ("Please forgive the trespass of your (maid-)servant" [v. 28]).[36] As David Reimer has noted, the fact that Abigail now explicitly asks David to forgive her trespass proves problematic for those who would maintain that Abigail cannot really be assuming blame in any meaningful way.[37] Indeed, notice what she might say but does not. She does not say "Please forgive the trespass of Nabal, my fool of a husband." It is, in fact, as Abigail has maintained from the beginning, her own trespass that she is asking David to forgive.[38] Moreover, the reuse of "maidservant" in vv. 27 and 28 confirms that David's acceptance of the delayed foodstuffs is integrally bound up with her plea to be forgiven for failing to ensure they arrived earlier.[39]

That Abigail cannot really be asking David to forgive her here might seem to be suggested by her initial focus on the advisability of leaving the

36. While V. Long suggests that in this context "presumption" (NIV) is a reasonable gloss for פשע (*1 and 2 Samuel*, 238), this and comparable translations (see esp. "boldness" [NJPS]) require both an exceptional softening of the usual meaning of this noun (see *HALOT* 2:981–82, s.v. פשע, which rightly favors "transgression") and the assumption that Abigail is simply being polite rather than actually asking for forgiveness—an interpretation for which evidence would appear to be lacking.

37. See Reimer, "Stories of Forgiveness," 371. Thus, McCarter is forced to insist that what Abigail really offers here is merely another "politeness" (i.e., "forgive me for speaking further"), without explaining why continuing her speech would require an apology or why the form of this "apology" is rather different from what is found in v. 24 or indeed 2 Sam 14 (*I Samuel*, 398). So too, Alter suggests that Abigail can only be "speaking as though the fault was hers," because the blame solely rests on her husband (*David Story*, 157). While he does not quite say so explicitly, Tsumura seems inclined to recognize that Abigail here is apologizing for more than merely speaking further (*First Book of Samuel*, 589).

38. Auld does not fully explain how Abigail's guilt relates to Nabal's, but he rightly sees Abigail's initial owning of the guilt and request to be forgiven of it here as more than merely rhetorical flourishes (*I & II Samuel*, 299).

39. If the provisions asked for by David were in a sense a debt owed to him by Nabal, then Abigail's eventual provision of them effectively paid that debt. What this transaction does not seem to do, however, is excuse the initial and rude withholding of this payment for which Abigail seeks to take responsibility by confessing her unintentional oversight. While David forgives her for what is by comparison a minor misdemeanor, and may effectively "forget" what Nabal has done by not taking vengeance himself, there is little sign of forgiveness of Nabal on David's part.

vanquishing of David's enemies (like Nabal) to the Lord, so as to avoid evil (v. 28) or grief or a guilty conscience for having shed blood without cause (v. 31). Of course, it is true that this is very much at the heart of Abigail's reasoning for why David must not kill Nabal, but what Abigail seems to be claiming is that her oversight in failing to keep an eye on her husband has led to a situation in which David has put himself in jeopardy by intending to repay a slight. While David's well-being and the fate of his house are indeed partly why Abigail urges David to forgive her, they are not the only reasons nor indeed perhaps as important for her as the one that she leaves him with at the end of v. 31: "And when the LORD has dealt well with my lord, then remember your (maid-)servant." Abigail first refers to herself explicitly as David's maidservant when taking the blame (v. 24) and then again when explaining what she had failed to do (v. 25). Having done so again in presenting the delayed food (v. 27) and in explicitly asking for forgiveness (v. 28), Abigail here refers to herself as his maidservant yet again, in asking that David forget about Nabal but remember her, after the Lord has taken care of David's enemies.

The suggestion that Abigail really is asking for forgiveness not for her husband, or even as a proxy for him, but for herself, for failing to keep an eye on her reckless husband, would seem to be confirmed by various aspects of David's response. While David "blesses" the Lord for sending her (v. 32), David also proceeds to bless Abigail herself for sparing him precisely the bloodguilt (and the taking of matters into his own hands) that she has warned him against (v. 26).[40] In v. 34, David may hint that Abigail's fault, rather than Nabal's, is the one he is forgiving, when he reaffirms to Abigail that the Lord has not merely *sent you*, but restrained me "from *hurting you*" (מהרע אתך [v. 34]).[41] Whether the hurt/evil that David in this verse claims he would have done to Abigail should be understood as the same lethal sort he would have inflicted on Nabal and his men, or merely a by-product of it, is not entirely clear. But David's reference to her fate and her survival is noteworthy and may well support the suggestion above that there was , indeed, something for him to forgive after all.

Why David will not now harm Abigail (or Nabal's house) is explained finally in v. 35 where David proceeds to take from her hand (מידה; rather than from Nabal's hand) the provisions she has brought and then invites

---

40. Jobling, *1 Samuel*, 155; Campbell, *1 Samuel*, 261.

41. Fokkelman is unable to account for this, calling it a "surprising object" (*Crossing Fates*, 514).

Abigail to "go up in peace to your house." While "go in peace" is of course a common dismissal formula in the Hebrew Bible, David's dismissal of Abigail in peace to her house recalls both David's allusion to the peace of Nabal, his house, and all that belongs to him (ואתה שלום וביתך שלום וכל אשר־לך שלום [v. 6]) in his initial overture to Nabal but also the quite lethal "evil" (הרעה) planned by David for all of Nabal's house (כל־ביתו), reported to Abigail in v. 17, when David's overture is rebuffed.[42] If David's dismissal here thus hints at forgiveness, his final words are still more telling. Admittedly, on their own, David's words in v. 35—"I have obeyed your voice" (שמעתי בקולך)—might refer to anything in Abigail's preceding speech, including her encouragement to spare Nabal. However, David's prefacing of these words with "See" (ראי) invites both her and the reader to consider what it is that she can see. While she may suspect that David will not now harm Nabal, the only thing she knows—the only thing she sees from David's words "Go to your house in peace"—is that David will indeed not harm her, as he might have. In considering what it is that Abigail has said that has prevented David from harming her (and encouraged him to allow her to go to her home in peace), it seems most likely to be Abigail's plea in v. 24 that David might forgive or, literally, "lift up" the transgression of "your maidservant." Thus, when David says to Abigail, in the final words of v. 35, "I will lift up your face" (ואשא פניך), he confirms that it is Abigail's request for forgiveness for her own minor failing that he has now granted.[43]

From all of this, it will be clear how I think the text invites us to answer the questions put forward at the outset: who appears to be forgiven, and of what do they seem to be forgiven? A close reading of the text suggests, I think, that Abigail does indeed take the blame and then secures from David the forgiveness for which she asks. Despite what many commentators have suggested, I find no evidence that Nabal has found forgiveness at all. Unlike Abigail, the reader finds no confession of guilt from Nabal nor remorse for or repentance of his offense. That may be neither here nor there. More crucially, there is no evidence within the narrative of a request from Nabal,

42. See, e.g., Exod 4:18; Judges 18:6; 1 Sam 1:17, 20:42, etc.

43. Fokkelman, sees her as "pardoned" without David speaking of transgression or forgiveness (*Crossing Fates*, 519). Klein recognizes that this signals the granting of her request, but does not specify which request (*1 Samuel*, 251). That the "lifting up of the face" represents a response to Abigail's petition is suggested by the reuse of נשא and (as Gordon notes [*I & II Samuel*, 186]) by the use of this same turn of phrase in Gen 32:20 (אולי ישא פני, "perhaps he will lift up my face") where Jacob, in preparing to meet the brother he has wronged, hopes that he will be forgiven.

or from Abigail, for Nabal's offense to be forgiven; nor, perhaps for this very reason, do we find David offering to do so. The reason why Nabal is not forgiven would appear to be that Abigail succeeds in persuading David that her comparatively trivial failure is the material and precipitating one and the one in need of being forgiven by him. That Nabal's offense remained unforgiven by David is suggested by David's exultation in v. 39 on hearing of the death of Nabal, whose demise he sees to be divine repayment for Nabal's insolence toward him.

Conclusion

If the above is found to be persuasive, and the only forgiveness to be found in 1 Sam 25 is found not by Nabal but Abigail, it would also seem that she was forgiven very little. Indeed, as we have seen, the "sin of omission" that she appears to confess—and for which she asks to be forgiven by David— would seem to pale almost absurdly beside her husband's offense, however trivial it is judged to be. In fact, we have argued that the story suggests this was precisely her aim and that her tactic was not merely sound but successful. While modern readers may be inclined to cringe at the need for Abigail to confess such a minor misdemeanor, it seems far more likely that Abigail's presentation of herself as a penitent and "saintly sinner" would have been seen by ancient readers as explaining—at least in part—not only why David married Abigail but also why she became known as a woman of "prudence" (טובת־שֹכל; 25:3).

5

Forgiven and Unforgiven
in the Book of Kings

David G. Firth

ALTHOUGH THE HEBREW BIBLE has a rich vocabulary associated with the forgiveness of sin,[1] comparatively little of it appears in the book of Kings. This may, to some extent, be because a key goal of the book is to explain why both Israel and Judah end up in exile, something that requires that neither be forgiven (or, at least, not until punishment is completed). Yet despite this, there are key points at which forgiveness emerges as a key theme, in particular through the use of the verb סלח. As is well known, this verb is only used with God as its subject in the Old Testament, so that as Olivier has observed, "the denotation of *slch* is an act of pardon by God alone."[2] More importantly for our purposes, it is important to note the centrality of the theme of forgiveness in Solomon's prayer (1 Kgs 8:22–53) and the

---

1. Principally associated with the roots סלח, כפר, and נשא, though, of course, forgiveness might be expressed through narration rather than depending on the presence of particular words. For example, in Isa 6:6, Isaiah's lips are touched with a coal from the altar, signaling forgiveness, though in this instance the forgiveness is also declared by the seraph.

2. Olivier, סלח, *NIDOTTE*, 3:260. See also Talstra, *Solomon's Prayer*, 192–201.

expectations it creates of forgiveness as a central theme in the book. In particular, the verb סלח occurs five times in this prayer (1 Kgs 8:30, 34, 36, 39, 50), making it a key theme in the prayer. Yet this focus on forgiveness needs to be contrasted with the few accounts of forgiveness in the book with only Naaman receiving forgiveness (2 Kgs 5:18), while Manasseh is said to have been denied forgiveness (2 Kgs 24:4). How then are we to integrate these elements, where forgiveness is apparently a central aspect of the temple, and yet in spite of its presence the only one whose forgiveness is recounted is in fact someone who is unable to enter it? What role, then, does the theme of forgiveness play in the book, and what light might it shed on its otherwise enigmatic conclusion (2 Kgs 25:27–30)? To explore this, a close reading of the motif of forgiveness in Solomon's prayer will first be provided. From this, the intratextual links the prayer provides will be developed in the Naaman and Manasseh narratives before providing a brief reflection on the possible significance of this for the book's conclusion.

The Prayer of Solomon (1 Kgs 8:22–53)

Solomon's prayer is a carefully presented piece that is integrated into its current position. In spite of the debates around the attitude of the narrator to Solomon in 1 Kgs 1–11,[3] all are agreed that the report of the prayer is carefully woven into the whole of 1 Kgs 1–11, though of course *how* it is thus integrated remains a matter of dispute.[4] It is not the purpose of this paper to resolve those disputes. However, it is perfectly possible in a narrative that is as subtle as Hays has proposed to offer points of genuine praise of Solomon, even if the final goal is his condemnation. That is, from the perspective of the compilers of the book of Kings, it is not necessary to commend all of Solomon's actions; indeed, it is perfectly possible to be highly critical of him overall,[5] while yet approving of a particular action. Hays has rightly pointed to hints even in 1 Kgs 8 of elements where Solomon is criticized

---

3. Compare Parker, "Solomon as Philosopher King?" and his presentation of Solomon as the ideal king with the more subtle readings of Olley, "Pharaoh's Daughter," and Hays, "Has the Narrator Come."

4. See Olley, "Pharaoh's Daughter," 357–59.

5. In addition to the wide-ranging observations of Hays, "Narrator," one should also note the prominence of Pharaoh's daughter. This is noted by Olley, finding her to be central to the whole presentation of Solomon ("Pharaoh's Daughter," 358).

for creating a misunderstanding of the temple.[6] But the fact that YHWH's glory fills the temple (1 Kgs 8:10–11) suggests that even with significant failings on Solomon's part, the temple is something that YHWH has approved, with the presence of his glory matching the filling of the tabernacle in Exod 40:34–38. That approval may well be limited. It is notable that in Lev 1:1, YHWH called to Moses from the tent that has just been filled with his glory, whereas YHWH will next appear to Solomon and warn him that the temple itself is no guarantee of divine favor since he requires faithfulness—abandoning him for other gods will lead to its destruction (1 Kgs 9:8). Nevertheless, although it may represent an imperfect act on Solomon's part, it can still represent "the high point of Solomon's rule."[7]

The prayer itself is presented as a carefully composed unit, consistent with a wider pattern of lists that Davies has noted, particularly through the use of seven-item elements or multiples thereof.[8] For example, within 1 Kgs 8, there are seven occurrences of the root קהל and a further twenty-one occurrences of בית. As such, the presence of seven clear petitions within the prayer is no surprise. With Schmid, we should separate vv. 22–30 from the remainder of the prayer as introductory petitions,[9] with the balance of the prayer seen as a single unit. The introduction, however, establishes the frame for interpreting the petitions. At the same time, we need to observe that there are variations to each petition, indicating that the different components required some changes in form. Doing so enables us to see the unity of the prayer as a whole while still recognizing the introductory nature of vv. 22–30. More importantly, it is in v. 30 that we have the first occurrence of סלח, with all the subsequent petitions flowing from this statement. This suggests that as each petition flows from this introduction to some extent, then forgiveness is an important element, even when the verb סלח does not appear in the petition, and that other elements can stand in place of this. However, when these other elements occur rather than סלח, there can be both condemnation of the guilty and vindication of the righteous.

6. Hays, "Has the Narrator Come," 167–69.

7. Wray Beal, 1 & 2 Kings, 132.

8. J. Davies, "Heptadic Verbal Patterns," esp. 26–27. This factor means that the argument of DeVries that petitions 6 and 7 are expansions (1 Kings, 120, 126) should be challenged. Whatever the exact link to Solomon, the literary form of the prayer was intended to contain seven petitions as part of this structure. See also Boda, Severe Mercy, 168–69, and Knoppers, "Prayer and Propaganda."

9. Schmid, Erste Buch der Könige, 237.

Once we accept the integrity of the prayer, the division into the main petitions following the introduction is generally agreed.[10] As with many public prayers, it is crafted with two audiences in mind—it is directed to YHWH, but rhetorically, it is also meant to address those present at the temple's inauguration (and through them, subsequent readers of this text).[11] Each new petition is marked by a phrase that indicates a shift to describe a new hypothetical possibility, with petitions commencing in vv. 31, 33, 35, 37, 41, 44, and 46. There is some evidence of patterning being used here, but it is not absolute, as can be seen in this table:

	Verse	Introductory Formula
Petition 1	8:31	את אשר יחטא איש
Petition 2	8:33	בהנגף
Petition 3	8:35	בהעצר
Petition 4	8:37	רעב כי־יהיה בארץ
Petition 5	8:41	וגם אל־הנכרי אשר לא־מעמך ישראל הוא
Petition 6	8:44	כי־יצא עמך למלחמה על־איבו
Petition 7	8:46	כי יחטאו־לך

It can be noted that petitions 1 and 7 are based on an imperfect of the verb חטא, one of the central verbs for sin in the Old Testament.[12] The shift here is from the singular to the plural, but this is because petition 1 is concerned with the action of an individual Israelite relative to other members of the community, whereas petition 7 reflects the concerns of the nation in battle. Petitions 2 and 3 are both linked by the use of a niphal infinitive construct with the preposition ב, a form well adapted to hypothetical cases. Petitions 6 and 7 are also linked by the repetition of the preposition כי in the initial position. Petitions 4 and 5 have looser introductory formulae, with

10. See B. Long, *1 Kings*, 101–2.

11. Cogan, *1 Kings*, 291.

12. Along with עון and פשע.

each reflecting a potential experience for which a prayer would be required, and that YHWH needed to hear from the temple.

A further element linking the petitions is the repetition of the phrase ואתה תשמע השמים (may you hear in heaven) as the start of the petitionary element (vv. 32, 34, 36, 39, 43, 45, and 49), though this is expanded with מכון שבתך (your dwelling place) in petitions 4, 5, and 7 (vv. 39, 43, and 49).[13] This expanded form points back to the introductory observation of v. 27, which noted that the highest heaven could not contain YHWH (הנה השמים ושמי השמים לא יכלכלוך), while v. 30 has also described heaven as YHWH's dwelling place. Alongside this, an emphasis on YHWH hearing in each petition emerges from the introduction, with various forms of the verb שמע occurring five times in vv. 28–30. Although a range of terms for prayer is used, the consistent emphasis is that YHWH needs to hear, with the last occurrence of שמע at the end of v. 30 coming immediately before the request for forgiveness with which the introduction concludes. All of this suggests that it is appropriate to read the prayer as a whole unit in the form in which we now find it, even if various levels of prehistory may have existed. However, one of the most striking features to note here is that Solomon presents the temple as a place where YHWH hears prayer, and this is the means for the forgiveness of sin rather than sacrifice.[14]

However, although the introduction has highlighted the need for YHWH to hear and forgive, we find the verb סלח in only four of the petitions.[15] It occurs in petitions 2 (v. 34), 3 (v. 36), 4 (v. 39), and 7 (v. 50). The terms associated with this distribution have also been noted by Talstra, who has pointed out that explicit language of sin (using the root חטא) occurs in these petitions. Talstra feels that this use of language is inconsistent, since the language of sin does not occur in the prayer's introduction,[16] but this does not take full account of the function of the introduction in framing the need for YHWH to hear and forgive as part of the prayer's rhetorical goal. Once this element is noted, then it can be seen that there is a close match between references to sin and forgiveness. Repentance (using

13. Kamp has demonstrated the value of reading this theme from the perspective of textual integrity ("Conceptualization," 434–38). He notes that the phrase מכון שבתך functions to point to a location "suitable for divine dwelling" (435).

14. Cf. Knoppers, "Prayer and Propaganda," 230.

15. Talstra has also noted that the verb סלח occurs only thirty-three times in Qal in the whole of the Old Testament (Solomon's Prayer, 192), so the five occurrences in this chapter represent a particularly high frequency.

16. Talstra, Solomon's Prayer, 195.

שׁוב) also occurs in petitions 2, 3, and 7, but is absent in petition 4. In this instance, the observation that YHWH knows the heart of the petitioner functions as something broadly equivalent. This is because the heart that YHWH knows is presumably penitent, given that the conditions that trigger the famine to which the petition refers derive from the sin of failing to be faithful to YHWH (Deut 28:21–22), whereas the goal of this famine is return to YHWH (cf. v. 40). As such, within Solomon's prayer, there is a close correlation between sin, repentance, and prayer, with YHWH asked to forgive sin when there is repentance and prayer.

It will be noted, however, that petitions 1, 5, and 6 do not mention forgiveness (סלח) directly. Does this mean that forgiveness is not relevant here? We can answer this only by noting the elements of these petitions. Petition 1 is the only one of these three to include direct mention of the language of sin (חטא). However, in this case, the issue addressed is not a sin that has required some punishment by YHWH but rather a dispute between two people where one has sinned against the other. In this instance, YHWH is (again) to hear, but this time his role is to act as judge. The implication of the fact that he is to vindicate one and condemn the other is that there is no repentance and that, therefore, the context that permitted divine forgiveness did not exist.[17] The overarching context established by v. 30 means that forgiveness remains a possibility for the condemned individual, but in the context of this petition, it remains only a possibility. Nevertheless, it makes clear that forgiveness is not automatic.[18]

Petitions 5 and 6 do not contain any of the vocabulary of sin, repentance, or forgiveness. However, the element of forgiveness remains because of the framing function of v. 30, not least because of the repetition of the call for YHWH to hear the prayers that are uttered. In petition 5, the focus is on the foreigner, in this case, the נכרי who is usually understood to be someone who is not only not an Israelite but someone who usually lived outside the land. That they might hear of YHWH (v. 42) certainly indicates that this is the class of foreigner intended. The renown of YHWH is said to be the trigger for their prayer, and YHWH is asked to do all that the

17. It should be noted that the prayer is concerned only with divine forgiveness. This petition assumes the need for interpersonal forgiveness, but as this is not the focus of the prayer, this issue is not addressed.

18. Brueggemann claims this establishes a contrast with the remaining petitions in that they seek the vindication of the unworthy (*1 & 2 Kings*, 111). However, although some contrast is present, the prayer's introduction suggests that a context for forgiveness still existed.

foreigner asks. This petition allows for a range of prayers, but if such people are to approach YHWH without having integrated themselves into Israel, then forgiveness would be an expected feature, though in effect their prayer might request any of the things noted in the other petitions. Petition 6 then focuses on the situation of Israel going into battle. Since Deut 28 had assumed that Israel's success in battle would depend on being in a proper relationship with YHWH (Deut 28:7), the summons to him maintaining Israel's cause (משפט) in the battle when he hears presumes that Israel's relationship with YHWH is appropriate for victory. A battle does not necessarily mean that Israel needed to repent, but the framing of this petition does allow for this possibility.

This evidence indicates that even in the petitions where forgiveness is not directly mentioned, it remains a possibility. However, the nature of the petitions that function this way means that other factors are involved, and forgiveness is not the only possible focus, whereas in the four where it is mentioned, the presence of sin means that forgiveness is the central focus. The prayer also allows the possibility that a foreigner might seek a relationship with YHWH because of his renown (by contrast, the queen of Sheba comes because of Solomon's renown [1 Kgs 10:1]), with the prayer's frame pointing to the possibility of forgiveness. Forgiveness is associated with repentance and prayer—and perhaps the most remarkable element here is that even though this is a prayer for the dedication of the temple (a place where sacrifices for sin could be offered), at no point does sacrifice feature in the discussion of sin and forgiveness. Rather, repentance and prayer are the key elements through which forgiveness for both the individual and the nation, the Israelite and the foreigner, are experienced as YHWH hears and responds.[19]

---

19. In passing, it is worth pointing to the conclusion of Talstra that whereas the other supposed "Deuteronomistic speeches" sought to justify the views of theodicy that justified the nation's punishment, this cannot be found here (*Solomon's Prayer*, 260). Indeed, as we shall note, within Kings, the perspective begins to point to hope beyond the nation's experience of exile. As Hobbs notes, prayer and repentance continue to provide hope (*1, 2 Kings*, 85). Against Nelson (*First and Second Kings*, 56), this chapter should not therefore be treated as a "primer of Deuteronomistic theology."

Naaman and Gehazi—Forgiven and Unforgiven (2 Kgs 5:1–27)

The prevalence of the language of forgiveness in Solomon's prayer might lead readers to expect that forgiveness would be an important theme in the stories that follow. But in fact, the language of forgiveness does not occur again until the Naaman story when Naaman asks for forgiveness for the fact that he needed to accompany the Aramean king when he worshipped Rimmon (2 Kgs 5.18). Although there is no formal record of this being given, that Elisha tells him to go in peace (שְׁלוֹם) would suggest that it is granted or at least anticipated, since the event for which forgiveness is sought is still future from Naaman's perspective within the story. More important for our purposes is that it can be shown that this story interacts with various petitions from Solomon's prayer.

Before we can comment on this element within the story, it is necessary to consider the form and structure of this story in order to demonstrate that within the final form of Kings, there are important intratextual links with multiple aspects of Solomon's prayer, all of which provide important background for this story, provided we understand the petitions of the prayer as various type scenes rather than as a comprehensive listing. There has been much debate about the unity of the story and the relationship of the various components,[20] but our concern here is simply to demonstrate the general coherence of the story as we have it, even if it may have derived from a range of sources. There is an immediately evident distinction between vv. 1–14, which constitute a miracle story, and vv. 15–27, which then contrast the responses of Gehazi and Naaman to this. Given the differences between Naaman and Gehazi, it is also possible to subdivide between vv. 15–19 and 20–27, treating them either as elements of one larger expansion of the miracle story or as two separate ones.[21] But against such divisions, Ngan has pointed to the prominence of the *Leitwort* שְׁלוֹם in vv. 19–27, as it is spoken in turn by each of Elisha (v. 19), Naaman (v. 21), and Gehazi (v. 22), though with a different sense each time.[22] Similarly, the story opens by noting Naaman's leprosy (v. 1)[23] and closes by noting Gehazi's (v. 27).

---

20. Ably summarized by Gilmour, *Juxtaposition and Elisha Cycle,* 144–46.

21. Cf. Cohn, "Form and Perspective," 171–72.

22. Ngan, "2 Kings 5," 589.

23. Although this is not a technical diagnosis, it continues to be used in discussion of texts like this, so is retained for pragmatic purposes.

Finally, the elements of significant amounts of gold and silver plus changes of clothes noted in v. 6 are taken up in vv. 22–23.[24] All of these elements could still be redactional, but they are sufficient to show that even if different elements were being brought together, the compilers of Kings have done so with some literary skill that justifies reading this chapter as a whole.[25]

As the story begins, we are told that YHWH had been granting victory to the Aramean forces in battle. Read in light of petitions 2 and 6 (1 Kgs 8:33–34, 44–45) we sense an immediate problem that faces Israel. Solomon's prayer encouraged Israel to pray for victory, but at this point YHWH has been giving victory to Israel's enemies, a situation that will not change until 2 Kgs 6:8—7:20. At this point, it is Aram and not Israel to whom YHWH has given victory in battle. Yet, there is an immediate though subtle hint that this is not the way things will continue, as the story then focuses on a little girl who has been captured in Israel and taken back to Aram where she has become a servant of Naaman's wife (לפני אשת נעמן). Aware of Naaman's condition, she expresses a wish to her mistress that Naaman could go to Samaria and encounter an unnamed prophet who was there, because this prophet would cure him. All this sets in motion a highly telescoped series of events that leads to the Aramean king sending Naaman to Samaria, complete with a letter requesting Israel's king to cure him of his illness. There is no need to think that the narrator approves of all the elements of the theology of the little girl or the kings of Aram and Israel. Indeed, where the girl attributes the healing power to the prophet, the story will make clear that it is YHWH who heals, even if the prophet might be involved. Even Elisha needs to be humbled in this story, because when he hears, he declares in v. 8 that Naaman should come to him so that he "might know there is a prophet in Israel" (וידע כי יש נביא ישראל).[26] This humbling comes most obviously when Naaman declares that he knows there is no God in all the earth save for Israel—Elisha had indicated that Naaman would reach a new level of knowledge, but that was to be focused on him. Instead, Naaman has come to know something about God that moves away from his previous position. Elisha is still a significant figure, but he is perhaps not as significant as he had thought.

---

24. C.f. B. Long, 2 Kings, 67–68.

25. Moore also points to the importance of גדול in the story, though as this is such a common word, it is probably best taken only as a subsidiary point (God Saves, 71–84).

26. C.f. Gilmour, Juxtaposition and Elisha Cycle, 154–55.

The change in Naaman thus prepares for a change in Israel's experiences in battle with Aram in the subsequent chapters and so represents a possible link to petitions 2 and 6. How YHWH was to bring about the change in Israel's military fortunes was not stated there, but this change begins here with a change in Naaman and, to a lesser extent, Elisha. But there is another more subtle connection with Solomon's prayer in v. 15 that should be noted. There we are told that Naaman "returned" to the man of God before making his declaration about Israel's God. The verb used here (שוב) is, of course, also a key verb for describing repentance and is used with the sense of repentance in each of petitions 2, 3, and 7. At one level, use of this verb here is simply an expected means of describing his movement from the Jordan back to Elisha, but it also prepares for the change in perspective he is about to bring as he declares that rather than discovering something about Elisha's identity, he has instead discovered that "there is no God in all the earth save for Israel" (ידעתי כי אין אלהים בכל־הארץ כי אם־ בישראל). His physical movement is thus matched by his change in theological perspective, and this in turn sets in chain a change in Israel's position in battle, suggesting that the national forgiveness that had been requested in petition 2 is about to begin.

The other link to Solomon's prayer here is with petition 5, which had focused on the foreigner (נכרי). The prayer assumes a situation where a foreigner prays because of hearing about YHWH's fame. Although Naaman does not here pray towards the temple as outlined within Solomon's prayer, he clearly fits the category of the foreigner who has heard of YHWH—it was reported to him through the little girl and is also directly evident in his healing (even if he was initially unimpressed by Elisha's healing technique). The context of his approach to Elisha requires some variations from the setting of Solomon's prayer, but that Elisha describes himself as one who stands before YHWH (חי יהוה אשר־עמדתי [v. 16]) certainly evokes a priestly role in the temple. As such, to the extent that Naaman is aware of what it means to worship YHWH, he is in the process of fulfilling the elements of petition 5, and his request for forgiveness can thus be seen in light of the prayer, so that he becomes the representative foreigner anticipated by the prayer whose request for forgiveness can be granted on the basis of repentance. With other figures in this story, Naaman's theology might be deficient in various ways, but repentance and a request for YHWH to forgive can lead to forgiveness.

Naaman's position stands, however, in marked contrast with Gehazi. Having decided that Naaman should indeed have paid a substantial sum and provided some clothing, he then goes after Naaman to claim them (v. 20). A theological neophyte, Naaman is more than happy to pay on the basis of Gehazi's story and, indeed, convinces Gehazi to take even more (vv. 22–23). Upon his return, Gehazi is confronted by Elisha. Like Naaman before him (v. 15), Gehazi also stood (עָמַד) before Elisha (v.25), though this time the outcome will be very different, as he is condemned by Elisha and so becomes a leper as Naaman had previously been. Gehazi's characterization here also stands in contrast to the young girl. Although limited, she had testified truly to what she knew, whereas there is no evidence that Gehazi's story about the visiting sons of the prophets is true. Indeed, the confrontation with Elisha (vv. 25–27) would have to take a very different form had Gehazi's story been true.

Although we later encounter Gehazi fit and well (2 Kgs 8:1–6), at the end of this story, at least, he stands in direct contrast to Naaman, suffering the affliction of the now forgiven Aramean. In that Solomon's prayer had primarily focused on the need for forgiveness, we also noted that petition 1 did not require that forgiveness be a key feature (though it remained possible). Rather, the focus there was on the need for YHWH to vindicate the righteous and condemn the wicked when one person had sinned against another. Gehazi has clearly sinned against Naaman through taking money and valuable clothing under false pretenses. Gehazi is therefore the one who is condemned. In this instance, there is no case brought to the temple as understood by the prayer. But the priestly role played here by Elisha creates a parallel to this setting, so that through him, YHWH does indeed condemn the wicked. That we later encounter Gehazi fit and well might suggest that this represents a different source, but if the connections to Solomon's prayer noted here are valid, then it suggests that even someone who is unforgiven may yet find forgiveness if there is repentance and prayer.

Manasseh—Unforgiven (2 Kgs 21:1–18)

The final direct reference to forgiveness occurs through the account of the reign of Manasseh and the direct comment on it that explains why he could not be forgiven (2 Kgs 24:1–5). The main text concerning Manasseh (2 Kgs 21:1–18) might be better described as a record than as a narrative, for though various actions of his are described, they are all presented as evidence that justifies the initial characterization of him as one who "did evil in YHWH's eyes" (ויעש הרע בעיני יהוה, 2 Kgs 21:2). What follows is in effect a catalogue of his sins, starting with an immediate contrast with Hezekiah when it is noted that he rebuilt the high places and then aligning him with Ahab. In that Hezekiah has been the only king to this point in the book to receive the wholly positive assessment that "he did what was right in YHWH's eyes" (2 Kgs 18:2),[27] while Ahab has been the standard point of comparison for anyone who has done evil, the compilers of Kings could not have been more thoroughly damning of Manasseh. He may have been Judah's longest reigning monarch, but his record of sins damns him. Indeed, by refraining from presenting any stories about Manasseh, it is almost as if the compilers of Kings have sought to prevent readers from having any sympathy for him. So, although his presentation cannot really be called a narrative in that there is no plot to resolve, the absence of story is itself a narrative decision that aims to create a distance between readers and Manasseh, so that his status as having done evil can be reinforced.

It is also worth noting that the evil he did is associated with worship practices and, in particular, the centrality of the temple as the place towards which prayer is to be directed as the place that represented YHWH's dwelling among his people. So, the charge sheet against Manasseh, which is outlined in vv. 3–9, is not about evil in the sense of what might today be thought of as crimes against humanity. Rather, his cultic transgressions were like the abominations of the nations (כתועבת הגוים) that YHWH had driven out from before Israel (2 Kgs 21:2), and it was his commitment to these that represented his evil. Manasseh in effect made Judah Canaanite through these practices while ignoring the temple, extending the pattern established by his grandfather Ahaz.[28]

The place of the temple as the proper place of worship is noted by an intrusive comment in vv. 7–8. Here, we have a citation of something YHWH is reported to have said to David and Solomon. Although most versions put this in quotation marks, treating it as a direct quote, it is difficult to find any one text that holds all these elements together. Rather, as is perhaps indicated by reporting that it was said to both David and Solomon, we are probably to understand this as an indirect citation, a drawing together of themes found in things that YHWH has said. These comments

27. Note how similar this statement is to the one about Manasseh, with only one crucial word changed: ויעש הישר בעיני יהוה.

28. Cf. Brueggemann, *1 & 2 Kings*, 533.

are focused on the elements of the choice of Jerusalem (and, in particular, the temple there) and that Israel need no longer wander out of the land, provided they do what YHWH has told them. One can immediately point to echoes of 2 Sam 7:6, 10, 13 and 1 Kgs 9:3 and 11:32. If so, the quote is intended as a drawing together of a range of texts that highlights the centrality of YHWH's commitment to the house of David and also to the house that he permitted Solomon to build. More particularly within the context of Kings, the echo with 1 Kgs 9:3 points readers back to Solomon's prayer in 1 Kgs 8:22–53, since this verse represents part of YHWH's response to the prayer. That the compilers of Kings were content to utilize indirect citations seems to be borne out by the fact that 2 Kgs 21:10–15 recounts a message from YHWH from "the prophets," though no prophets are named for Manasseh's reign. The presence of this feature in one part of the account makes it likely that we will have it repeated elsewhere. A striking feature of this prophetic judgment is that it demonstrates that it was Manasseh's own sin (v. 11b) that led to the sin of the nation (v. 11c), before finally noting the sin of the people on their own.[29]

This literary background suggests that once again Solomon's prayer is part of the textual world against which we are to read this account. Moreover, when we do so, we can easily see how Manasseh's actions are contrary to the content of the prayer, especially its introduction (1 Kgs 8:22–30). The seven petitions are less relevant here, because none of the conditions of the petitions arise. However, Manasseh's acts evoke several elements from the prayer's introduction. In particular, we can observe that even in Solomon's opening words, he alludes back to 2 Sam 7:1–17 in noting that there would continue to be a descendant of David on the throne, provided those descendants walk before YHWH. The opening statement in 2 Kgs 22:2 has already indicated that Manasseh has not done this, while his Canaanite practices are all presented as clear evidence that substantiates this. All of this indicates that Manasseh has no right to claim any promises associated with the Davidic covenant.

Further, it can be noted that the key elements in Solomon's prayer are that the possibility of forgiveness was established by repentance, prayer, and a positive attitude to the temple as the place that represented YHWH's dwelling place. But as is clear from the composite citation in vv. 7b–8, Manasseh has transgressed this. Rather than seeking YHWH, he has followed a range of practices that are designed to inquire of other deities while

29. Wray Beal, 1 & 2 Kings, 489–90.

ignoring the temple as the place where YHWH has agreed to have his name dwell. Solomon had acknowledged that the temple could not truly contain YHWH (1 Kgs 8:27), but even so, the temple was understood as the key representation of this dwelling. By filling the temple with elements associated with the worship of other deities, Manasseh had thus turned away from the means by which forgiveness might actually be achieved. It is this sin that ultimately leads the nation away from YHWH (vv. 9, 16), and it is this that finally leads to the sort of actions that modern readers are more likely to regard as evil (v. 16). By explicitly removing the potential to obtain forgiveness, Manasseh (and, through him, Judah) are placed in a position where they cannot obtain it.

This material then provides some of the background to the statement in 2 Kgs 24:3–4. There, it is said that YHWH would not forgive (סלח) Judah. It is notable that when referring to his sins, we now refer back only to 2 Kgs 21:16 and the statement about the innocent blood that he had shed. Manasseh's actions led to a removal of the possibility of forgiveness because the mechanisms that allowed it—repentance and prayer that recognized the temple—had gone. Josiah could not end this (2 Kgs 22:16–17), because his actions could not finally ensure that this was reversed, and the final kings of Judah merely followed a pattern Manasseh established instead. It is not that forgiveness was impossible—rather, the conditions necessary for forgiveness were not present. Manasseh is like Gehazi at the end of the Naaman story, and Judah in turn follows this pattern—they have removed themselves from the possibility of forgiveness. Nevertheless, the conditions established by Solomon's prayer continue.[30]

Conclusion

Within the book of Kings, therefore, we find those who are forgiven and those who are unforgiven. In understanding this, Solomon's prayer stands as a key element—part of a textual world in which we are to read the final form of the book. Crucially, it establishes the possibility of forgiveness, despite a range of sins, through prayer directed to the temple as the representative site of YHWH's presence, with repentance as the central requirement. Prayer and not sacrifice is the means by which forgiveness is obtained, when that prayer is matched with repentance.

30. It is beyond the scope of this paper to address this, but the presentation of Manasseh in 2 Chr 33:1–20 seems to have read his story along these lines.

All of this begins to shed at least some light on the brief note of Jehoachin's release in 2 Kgs 25:27–30. Scholars have long struggled to know what to make of this since while it is something reported, like much of the reign of Manasseh, no real narrative is provided. Without attempting to offer a comprehensive account, it seems that Jehoachin's release allowed some of the conditions of Solomon's prayer to be resolved, even when no temple was standing. But as the temple could not fully contain the God, this was not an insurmountable problem, since prayer was ultimately directed to God through the temple. Rather, readers see that if there is repentance and prayer, forgiveness may yet be possible. If it is not finally a definite word of grace, it perhaps allows readers to hope that one might not be far away.

6

Forgiveness as the Mitigation of Punishment in Kings

Repentance, the Monarchy, and Divine Motive

J. Michael Thigpen

Introduction

This study explores the intersection of two longstanding lines of inquiry. The first is the meaning of the book of Kings and its relationship to the other parts of the Old Testament canon. The second is the question of the nature and significance of repentance. This study does not seek to solve the perennial questions related to Kings or to affirm or reject a particular past solution. Neither will this exploration examine repentance in all its fullness in the Old Testament. Rather, this inquiry will analyze the effect of repentance and its relationship to YHWH's motives and intentions, suggesting that repentance in Kings is not salvific but rather mitigatory. That is to say, the merciful acts of forgiveness with which YHWH responds to acts of repentance are anticipatory, partial, and pedagogical. Such an understanding of repentance in Kings coheres with a prominent theme in Jeremiah and Ezekiel. In these prophets, the explicit statements of YHWH's motive indicate that rather than being motived by repentance to save, YHWH is motivated to grant repentance as part of the new covenant.

67

Together, these themes provide another avenue of understanding the hope expressed by the book of Kings and the mechanism of hope brought forth in the prophets. They also help the canonical reader situate the function and significance of repentance in the book of Kings.

The Meaning of the Book of Kings

McConville offers a helpful starting place for considering the meaning of the book of Kings. The book addresses the "loss of identity, of which loss of" the land and temple represent the utter depths of the judgment the nation faces.[1] Although Solomon may rightly be seen as the "peak of the monarchy's achievement," the hints of impending doom placed prior to his request for wisdom and the tales of his renown prepare the reader to understand that "there could be no permanent salvation for Israel in a Solomon."[2]

The specter of failure and the promise of hope come together most prominently in Solomon's dedicatory prayer. There the reader is reminded that there is no one who does not sin (1 Kgs 8:46) but that there is hope even after the devastating punishment of exile (1 Kgs 8:46–53). Once again, however, there are clues here that the hope is not as straightforward as it may seem.

The successful petition for forgiveness is one in which the people confess their sin and, more specifically, their "rebellion against the known will of God."[3] In addition to recalling the language of Deut 6, for the canonical reader, it rules out petitions like those of Judg 10:10–16 where the people show up with idols in hand seeking deliverance from YHWH, who promptly refuses their half-hearted approach.[4] It also brings to mind the significant theme of the heart in Jeremiah and Ezekiel, for it is the heart that is incurably deceitful and sick (Jer 17:9). It is the heart that is evil and stubborn (Jer 3:17; 5:23–24; 7:24; 9:24; 11:8; 13:10; 16:12; 17:1; 18:12; 23:17; Ezek 2:4; 3:7; 14:3) and that must be cleansed from evil for there to be

---

1. McConville, "Narrative and Meaning," 34.

2. McConville, "Narrative and Meaning," 35–36. For further analysis of the literary foreshadowing of Solomon's demise, see Hays, "Has the Narrator Come."

3. J. Gray, *I & II Kings*, 228.

4. There is some debate over whether the Israelites' repentance in Judg 10:10–16 is genuine but fleeting or if it is merely self-serving. I find the arguments of Block, Webb, and, more recently, Hoyt to be persuasive. See Block, *Judges, Ruth*, 348–49; Webb, *Book of Judges*, 44–48; Hoyt, "In Defense," 204–8. For a recent argument for reading true repentance in Judg 10, see Frolov and Stetckevich, "Repentance in Judges."

salvation (Jer 4:14; 24:7; Ezek 18:31). It is the heart that must be circumcised (Jer 4:4; 9:26; 31:33; Ezek 18:31; 36:26) so that the people will seek YHWH wholeheartedly (Jer 29:13; 32:39–40; Ezek 11:19).[5]

Although the individual sin of each monarch can be set aside as his failure, the ultimate impotence of each instance of repentance raises the question of whether the lack of lasting spiritual reform is the result of each king's "personal inadequacy to the moment . . . or whether there is in fact little hope of permanent betterment for Judah through reform of the cult—even if such reform *is* an absolute requirement of the deuteronomic law."[6] This question climaxes in the reform of Josiah and the shocking notice that, despite Josiah's dedication to obedience and repentance, "the sentence on Judah uttered over Manasseh still stands."[7] The question is whether YHWH's act of mitigation is to be understood as forgiveness.[8]

McConville's conclusion regarding the succession of failed reforms is this: "Far from leading the reader consistently to expect salvation for Judah through a Davidic king, it leads him rather to expect the opposite. With the reforming kings there was an intensifying insistence that Reform did not in fact produce the desired results."[9] The instruction to repent is given as the key to salvation, but actual instances of repentance fail to produce the necessary lasting reform. So "there is much in Kings that expresses a theology of grace, and that in itself leaves a door ajar for some new thing to happen in the relationship between God and his chosen people."[10] The key question is what is the role of repentance in Kings' "theology of grace"? McConville suggests that Solomon's prayer indicates that exile is not the final word and that "repentance is clearly an important precondition of salvation."[11]

In a 2001 article, Gershon Galil analyzed the theme of repentance in the book of Kings and insightfully noted that "it is not coincidental that repentance is expressed in the book through wicked kings and their sins:

---

5. For a survey of the theme of the people's heart in Jeremiah, especially in comparison to YHWH's heart, see Thigpen, *Divine Motive*, 178–82.

6. McConville, "Narrative and Meaning," 42.

7. McConville, "Narrative and Meaning," 44.

8. Lambert asks a similar question. "God sets out to destroy the nation. Moses intercedes, and YHWH declares: 'I have forgiven, as you asked' (Num. 14:20). Immediately thereafter, he condemns the present generation to death (Num. 14:21–23). How does that constitute forgiveness?" Lambert, *How Repentance Became Biblical*, 48.

9. McConville, "Narrative and Meaning," 45.

10. McConville, "Narrative and Meaning," 46.

11. McConville, "Narrative and Meaning," 48.

through Jeroboam and, specifically, through Ahab."[12] Like McConville, Galil ultimately sees a message of hope in the book of Kings, and he understands that hope to be congruent with the basic outlines of hope in Deuteronomy and Jeremiah.[13]

The results of this study are largely in agreement with McConville and Galil. There is a theology of hope in Kings. "The author of Kings viewed the relationship between God and Israel as an everlasting bond. Even though the Israelites continually betrayed Him . . . God would remain attentive and forgiving."[14] However, the relationship between repentance and forgiveness, between repentance and salvation, needs further exploration. McConville helpfully demonstrates how Kings sets up the reader to expect that the repentance of individual monarchs will never yield lasting spiritual fruit. Galil insightfully highlights that wicked kings display repentance. Surely this must encourage readers that if YHWH responded favorably to the repentance of wicked kings, he would welcome their repentance. Yet the question of permanent and lasting change—salvific change—remains.[15] Is YHWH motivated *by repentance* to save? Is wholehearted repentance within the reach of the people? Can any repentance be more effective than that of Hezekiah or Josiah?

Similar questions arise when the reader considers the tensions in Deuteronomy, Jeremiah, and Ezekiel where the people are commanded to reform their hearts (Deut 10:16; Jer 4:4, 14; Ezek 18:31) but also to expect that it would be God himself who would act on their hearts (Deut 30:6; Jer 24:7; 31:33; 32:39–40; Ezek 11:19; 36:26).[16]

Repentance in the Old Testament

There has been a recent resurgence in the study of repentance in the Old Testament. Lambert has sought to address the question of repentance

12. Galil, "Message of the Book," 409.

13. For important nuances that may distinguish the messages of Deuteronomy and Jeremiah, see McConville, *Judgment and Promise*, and McConville, "1 Kings 8:46–53." Nevertheless, although these books may have various textural differences, the fundamental theology expressed in them is harmonious, though not identical.

14. Galil, "Message of the Book," 410.

15. A subsequent section will explore Freitheim's helpful discussion of conversion versus renewal perspectives in Kings.

16. See McConville's assessment of the literary connections between these books and the theme of the heart ("1 Kings 8:46–53," 367–68).

broadly, taking a materialist viewpoint and questioning whether what we see in the Old Testament is actually repentance as understood in contemporary theological terms—an interior act of contrition for sin expressed externally.[17] Broadly speaking, Lambert concludes that a careful materialist reading of the matter yields an understanding that many instances that have traditionally been viewed under the rubric of repentance in the Old Testament are not actually repentance—internal penitential recognition and response—but rather might be better viewed as material responses to distress, petitions for relief, or a turning to YHWH, not a return to a prior relational state from which the individual had departed.

With regard to the book of Kings, Lambert gives penetrating attention to Ahab's response to the announcement of impending doom in 1 Kgs 21. Noting that many commentators "interpret the act of which God approves, submission . . . , to be a quasi-technical term for an internal penitential state," the textual details do not support such a reading.[18] Boda's assessment supports Lambert's conclusions: "Prayer and repentance are . . . not the only ways to avert or bring an end to punishment . . . . Ahab responds with *rites of humility.* . . . Yahweh sees his humility . . . and spares Ahab's generation."[19] Several questions remain unanswered in Lambert's analysis. Even if Ahab's acts are not acts of true repentance, what is their literary function in the book of Kings? How does the divine act towards Ahab in response to his self-humiliation fit with the other gracious of acts of YHWH in the book? And finally, is the interior, the heart, uninvolved in these acts and in YHWH's intentions? To answer these, I will explore the context of the mitigation of punishment in Kings, its role in the book, and potential connections to matters of the heart addressed in the New Covenant.

17. Lambert, *How Repentance Became Biblical.* It is beyond the scope of this study to engage Lambert's entire project directly. Although Lambert's work demonstrates the need for a closer and more attentive reading of the texts to account for what actually transpires, I remain unconvinced of his rejection of the presence of repentance as an interior act that is found widely in the Old Testament. As such, this study continues to use the traditional terminology of repentance for positive responses to announcements of judgment, distinguishing true repentance, wholehearted repentance, from other acts intended to sway YHWH. The broad basis for this stance will become clearer as the study progresses. I do readily acknowledge (and point out below) cases in my past writing where my language was not sufficiently nuanced, and repentance terminology was used too widely and without clear distinction. Lambert's careful and attentive analysis has been very useful in this regard.

18. Lambert, *How Repentance Became Biblical*, 21.

19. Boda, *Severe Mercy*, 183.

More narrowly, a conversation on the nature of repentance and forgiveness in the book of Judges has emerged in the publications of Hoyt and of Frolov and Stetckevich.[20] Key questions that have arisen in their conversation have helped to guide this inquiry. Much of the disagreement is whether to take any positive act in response to the announcement of judgment or the distress of punishment as an act of repentance, and whether an act of deliverance by YHWH indicates that genuine repentance has occurred. Finally, as Hoyt wisely notes, in addressing these complex issues, we must be cautious to carefully distinguish "between deliverance from a physical situation and 'salvation' in the sense of forgiveness or blessings."[21] Together with the questions prompted by Lambert's work, we can now survey the role of repentance in the book of Kings.

Repentance in Kings

Repentance in 1 Kgs 8

Within Solomon's dedicatory prayer, we see the covenant curses (Deut 28:15–68) of foreign oppression (1 Kgs 8:33–34), drought (1 Kgs 8:35–36), famine, pestilence, and plague (1 Kgs 8:37–40) reversed by acts of repentance that prompt a merciful response from YHWH, including forgiveness (סלח), (1 Kgs 8:34, 36, 39), hearing (1 Kgs 8:34, 36, 39), return (שׁוב) from exile (1 Kgs 8:34), teaching the people the good way (1 Kgs 8:36), and the rendering of true justice informed by YHWH's knowledge of each individual's heart (1 Kgs 8:39).

Each of these scenarios is not presented as a one-time historical event that will be faced, but rather as a potentially repeating palette of covenant discipline and forgiveness that the people may face. The theological power of this section, "the heaping up of future conditions," is intensified by "the remarkable use of the number seven. The central prayer contains seven petitions" and "the wordplays on 'repent' and 'carry into captivity' (שׁוב, שׁבה) involve seven shifts of perspective back and forth, from sin to repentance."[22]

---

20. See Hoyt, "Reassessing Repentance in Judges"; Frolov and Stetckevich, "Repentance in Judges"; and Hoyt, "In Defense."

21. Hoyt, "In Defense," 209.

22. B. Long, 1 Kings, 104.

It is important to note that within this section, only 1 Kgs 8:40 and 43 contain an explicit citation of YHWH's motives.[23] There are no express motive clauses that YHWH should forgive "because of" the people's repentance. Rather, Solomon's prayer indicates that the acts of repentance serve as the occasion for YHWH to act; that his actual motive for acting might be that the people, in response to his mercy, would fear him (1 Kgs 8:40); and that in the case of his response to a foreigner's appeal, that his name might be known and feared among all people, not just Israel (1 Kgs 8:43).

Similarly, in 1 Kgs 8:46–53, only two explicit motive statements are found. Neither of them indicates that YHWH should be motivated by repentance. Rather, the motive clauses found in 1 Kgs 8:51 and 53 cite YHWH's redemption of Israel from Egypt and his election of them to be his unique people as reasons for him to move their captors to have compassion on them. These two motives should not be thought of as disparate but rather cooperative. YHWH chose Israel and brought them out of Egypt, and in light of those prior actions, YHWH should be motivated to act compassionately now.[24] This observation accords with the accounts of YHWH's gracious acts towards Jehoahaz and Jeroboam II. As McConville notes, "YHWH's intervention . . . in the reigns of Jehoahaz and Jeroboam II . . . is not motivated by any righteousness on the part of the two kings," but rather resembles his "interventions in the time of the judges . . . the reason for salvation is simply, and very generally, YHWH's promised commitment to Israel."[25] Though McConville does not cite them, both of these accounts have an explicit statement of divine motive. In 2 Kgs 13:4, the reader is told that YHWH acts in response to Jehoahaz's entreaty because he saw the plight of the people under the oppression of Syria. That the divine motive is YHWH's compassion for the people is confirmed in 2 Kgs 13:22–23 where we find the summary statement that "the LORD showed them favor and had compassion on them, and he turned toward them, because of his covenant with Abraham, Isaac, and Jacob."[26] Similarly, in 2 Kgs 14:27, YHWH's observation of the people's affliction and his decision not to blot out their

---

23. For a survey and analysis of divine motive in the Old Testament, see Thigpen, *Divine Motive*.

24. For the concept of cascading or nested motives see Anscombe, *Intention*, 46. For an exploration of cascading motives in the Old Testament, see Thigpen, *Divine Motive*, 60–63.

25. McConville, "Narrative and Meaning," 47.

26. All translations are the author's own unless otherwise noted.

name is the basis of the improvement of their conditions during the reign of Jeroboam II.

Repentance and the Mitigation of Punishment in Kings

The announcement of YHWH's decision to punish Solomon's idolatry is accompanied by a note of mitigation. YHWH will not take the kingdom away from Solomon entirely. Instead, he will tear away only a portion of the kingdom. The decision to mitigate the punishment is expressly motivated by YHWH's regard for David (לְמַעַן דָּוִד) and the city of Jerusalem (וּלְמַעַן יְרוּשָׁלַ͏ִם) that he had chosen. This early mitigation sets the tone for the gracious acts to follow. The attenuation of the punishment is not based on repentance but on God's regard for his past choices and his faithfulness to his prior promises.[27]

In 1 Kgs 13, we encounter the account of Jeroboam's punishment and YHWH's positive response to the entreaty of the man of God. No repentance on the part of Jeroboam is recorded, and Jeroboam is noted as having continued in his idolatrous ways (1 Kgs 13:33–34). Jeroboam's encounter with the man of God and his subsequent punishment and healing were "a sign of what" might happen if Jeroboam would seek YHWH.[28] The immediate punishment is undone, but the ultimate demise of his kingdom is still yet to come.

> The most intriguing use of divine approval as a motive is in 1 Kgs 21:29, which relates YHWH's response to Ahab's repentance. There are two key factors that make this text remarkable. The first, is that this is the first occurrence of divine approval of an individual's repentance as a motive for a divine action. The second is that the subject of the divine approval is Ahab.[29]

A few details in this noteworthy account are significant. First, as noted above, repentance language (שׁוּב) is not used of Ahab. Rather, Ahab adopts all of the appropriate rites of mourning in response to the overwhelming

---

27. House, *1, 2 Kings*, 168.

28. Leithart, *1 & 2 Kings*, 99.

29. Thigpen, *Divine Motive*, 68. By first, I mean the first encountered in the canonical sequence. I should note that if I were writing the quoted section now, I would, in light of Lambert and Hoyt, be more cautious with the use of repentance language for Ahab's actions. The overall evaluation still stands, but the language could be significantly more precise and nuanced.

announcement of judgment. "His duty of mourning . . . was not a private precaution only, but a public duty, to avert the potential harm."[30] Ahab's humility "is his most positive act in the book," but he "does not fully learn how to listen to God and God's messenger."[31] Ahab's positive response does not fully negate YHWH's judgment, but it does mitigate it by postponing it.

The next occurrence of this pattern of repentance and mitigation is seen in 2 Kgs 11 and the story of Jehoash that was surveyed earlier in the study. Punishment was mitigated by YHWH without acts of repentance.

Like Ahab, Hezekiah does not repent in light of the threat of destruction by Sennacherib. He adopts the appropriate mourning rites, tearing his cloths, wearing sackcloth, and entreating YHWH for relief (2 Kgs 19:1), demonstrating a posture of "utter humility before God."[32] YHWH's response via the prophet is direct and reassuring. Like Ahab, Hezekiah's humble response to impending doom has been well received.

The next episode of Hezekiah's story bears some resemblance to Jeroboam's in 1 Kgs 13. Here we find Hezekiah not seeking forgiveness following repentance but healing following entreaty.[33] Intriguingly, the explicit motive for YHWH's granting of Hezekiah's plea is theocentric. YHWH will act "for his own sake" (לְמַעֲנִי) and "for the sake of David my servant" (וּלְמַעַן דָּוִד עַבְדִּי) (2 Kgs 20:6).[34] "Proffered deliverance, however, can be qualified or even withdrawn. Hezekiah's dealings with Merodach-baladan in the immediately following section will dim, but not extinguish, the flame of Hezekiah and the hopes of Judah's exiled remnant."[35]

Josiah's story brings the theme of repentance and mitigation to a head. Like Ahab and Hezekiah, Josiah adopts the appropriate rites of mourning in light of the reading of the book of the Law (2 Kgs 22:11). However, in Josiah's narrative, we see an affirmation of much more than lament, mourning, and entreaty. YHWH affirms through Huldah that Josiah's heart was indeed soft, that he was truly humble (2 Kgs 22:19).[36] This kind of evaluative

30. J. Gray, *I & II Kings*, 444.

31. House, *1, 2 Kings*, 233–34.

32. Cohn, *2 Kings*, 133. Here Lambert on the act of appeal as a potentially separate phenomenon from repentance is insightful. See Lambert, *How Repentance Became Biblical*, 33–60.

33. For literary connections between the two stories, see Cohn, *2 Kings*, 140.

34. On the relationship between divine actions taken "for the sake of David" and theocentric motives, see Thigpen, *Divine Motive*, 67–68.

35. B. Long, *2 Kings*, 241.

36. Although Lambert, *How Repentance Became Biblical*, mentions Josiah in a few

language is not seen with any other king. This might lead the reader to expect that the fundamental situation might change—that disaster might be averted for the nation. Yet the penitent heart of Josiah results only in a delay in judgment that allows Josiah to avoid having to endure the inevitable destruction.

The juxtaposition of Judah's most penitent king and the coming judgment is striking in 2 Kgs 23:24–27. Whereas most summative accounts of the kings include a restrictive statement of failure (רק), Josiah's summary includes an expansive account of his true reform in 2 Kgs 23:24 (גם).[37] He is assessed positively against all the kings who had come before him (2 Kgs 23:25), and most importantly, Josiah alone is said to have responded with all his heart and soul, the very language of Solomon's prayer in 1 Kgs 8:48. Despite this parade example of true wholehearted repentance, the narrative goes on to affirm that the destruction of the nation is unavoidable (2 Kgs 23:26–27). The sins of Manasseh were too great and YHWH was unwilling (אבה) to pardon them (2 Kgs 24:3–4). This nexus of wholehearted repentance and divine unwillingness pushes the reader to consider the relationship between judgment, repentance, and forgiveness.

Repentance and Divine Motive on Mt. Carmel

I have waited until after the review of repentance and mitigation in Kings to address repentance in 1 Kgs 18. Although this narrative does not involve mitigation of punishment, it does help to connect the themes of repentance and divine motive in Kings to a broader theology of repentance and divine motive in the prophets that will be explored in the next section.

Space constraints prohibit an extensive exploration of 1 Kgs 18. For the purposes of this study, the focus will have to rest narrowly on 1 Kgs 18:36–40. The primary interpretive difficulties are found in 1 Kgs 18:37. In particular, there is a sharp debate over whether the phrase הסבת את־ לבם אחרנית (you turned their heart backwards) should be understood as a statement of divinely caused repentance or as a punitive act whereby YHWH had, prior to the Mt. Carmel event, turned the hearts of the people toward Baal. Much of the debate is driven by disagreements over how to

---

notes and alludes to Josiah in a discussion of Ahab, there is very little direct engagement with this story, and no attention is given to the heart language in 2 Kgs 22 or to that which is featured so prominently in the Solomon narratives.

37. The restrictive (רק) clauses occur in: 1 Kgs 3:2, 3; 2 Kgs 12:3; 14:4; and 15:4, 35.

understand the syntax of the passage and whether the perfect, הסבת, refers to an event prior to the narrative or to an event in the future, but after YHWH's miraculous fulfillment of Elijah's request.[38] Fishbane asserts, "There is nothing that justifies construing it with a future orientation (viz., if God responds, He will thereby turn the human heart to Him). Accordingly, it appears that the biblical phrase regards God as the cause of the peoples' sin and that just this is the offensive comment of Elijah."[39] More forcefully, he writes that translating the verb הסבת with reference to an imminent future act of repentance "violently offends the syntax of the passage, separating the verb from its following object."[40]

I would agree with Fishbane that a past tense reading is more natural than a future reading. However, the question that should be asked regarding the function and translation of הסבת is not whether it is past or future, but what is the temporal point of reference for the verb? Perfect verbs "often refer to events that happened *prior to a point y*."[41] So what is the *point y* for this perfect? I would suggest that the most natural reading of the narrative is that the *point y* is the miracle that will be in the immediate past when the Israelites realize that YHWH is indeed God, not Baal. They will look *back* to that now immediately past event and rightly conclude that it was YHWH who turned their hearts back, via the miracle, to recognize him. It is from the perspective of Elijah a yet future event, but from the hearers' perspective, their knowing and their recognition of the miracle as the event that opened their eyes will come *after* the miracle, thus making sense of the perfect form despite the action taking place in the future from Elijah's perspective. Although the reading suggested by McKenzie, Fishbane, and Cogan is plausible, I fail to see, and they do not elucidate, how their reading would function in the larger narrative structure of Kings. If, as argued above, the motive for forgiveness is not repentance itself, but rather YHWH's own character and initiative, then this narrative, read as a repentance prompted by the miraculous response to Elijah's request, fits within the trajectory of thought in Kings. Here is a striking example of a merciful act of YHWH that is unmerited but that results in repentance. This reading also helps connect this passage with other recognition events in the Old Testament

---

38. For discussion, see McKenzie, *1 Kings 16—2 Kings 16*, 123–35; Cogan, *1 Kings*, 43; and Brichto, *Toward a Grammar*, 139.

39. Fishbane, *Haftarot*, 96.

40. Fishbane, *Haftarot*, 349n12.

41. Van der Merwe et al., *Biblical Hebrew Reference Grammar*, 157.

and with the understanding of the relationship between repentance and salvation in Jeremiah and Ezekiel.

Reading the phrase as referring to the people's recognition of YHWH's miraculous intervention does fit with the pattern of recognition events in the Old Testament. As Zimmerli notes in reference to this passage, "Recognition is not just the illumination of a new perspective; it is a process of acknowledgment that becomes concrete in confession and worship and leads directly to practical decisions."[42] Note that the response is not "just" a new perspective. This means it is not less than a new perspective, and that it does include both interior change and an outward expression of that change.

Zimmerli's understanding runs contrary to Lambert's assessment that the incident at Carmel is not educational or reforming but a merely "physiological response to YHWH's overwhelming exhibition of power."[43] Although it is possible to read this event solely through the lens of power, this does not cohere well with the overall meaning and function of the statement of introduction and the statement of recognition. These are inherently pedagogical in that they are intended as self-introduction, and they are intended to prompt an appropriate response in light of the newly revealed knowledge of who YHWH is.[44]

It must be noted, even if we adopt a reading of 1 Kgs 18 that YHWH led the people to repentance with the miracle, there was no lasting effect. Sin continues virtually unabated after this short-lived return to YHWH. And yet, mercy continues in the ensuing chapters. YHWH continues to respond graciously, even to a king like Ahab. How are canonical readers to understand this?

Repentance and Divine Motive in the Prophets

"The former prophets understood that repentance is possible, finally, only because of God's promise; indeed, repentance is not possible without the promise being understood as directly applicable to the one who would repent."[45] This perspective, which Fretheim states so clearly, is borne out by the motive statements in the prophets regarding repentance and its relationship to salvation.

42. Zimmerli, "Knowledge of God," 67.
43. Lambert, How Repentance Became Biblical, 108.
44. Thigpen, Divine Motive, 81, 134; Zimmerli, "Knowledge of God," 142.
45. Fretheim, "Repentance in Former Prophets," 32.

When considering repentance as divine motive, it is largely absent as a motivation for salvation. In Jeremiah, despite his frequent calls for repentance and the prevalence of repentance vocabulary, especially שׁמע (listen), and שׁוב (turn back), "it is striking how infrequently these are actually identified as divine motives. Lack of repentance is a frequent motive for judgment, but actual repentance is virtually missing as a motive for salvation. It may be that like Ezekiel, Jeremiah's message is that this missing human response requires divine initiative."[46] Like Jeremiah, when divine motive is considered in Ezekiel, repentance is only minimally present as a motivation for salvation.[47]

Instead, what the reader finds is that rather than YHWH being motivated to save by acts of repentance, the motive statements of Jeremiah and Ezekiel and the overall theological trajectories of the two books indicate that "YHWH's desire to produce repentance" in his people "is the motive for divine action."[48] This is seen most clearly in the repentance language of walking (הלך), keeping (שׁמר), and obeying/listening (שׁמע), which are all part of what God will provide in the new covenant (Jer 31:31; Ezek 11:20; 36:25–27). The new covenant also provides for a deep relationship with YHWH, knowing him, in a way that his people needed, but which had been elusive for them to this point (Jer 31:34). Sprinkle assess the situation similarly:

> What was previously held out as a conditional promise—"the person who does these things will live by them"—is now in the age of restoration replaced by divine causation. Israel will indeed walk in the "statutes and ordinances" of Yahweh, albeit through a different agency. The "life" therein will be gained by spiritual revivification.[49]

Acts of repentance do show in motive clauses related to salvation, but most often they appear in "פֶּן clauses. As such they are given as motives that would bring about a change in YHWH's planned actions"[50] but only hypothetically. Similar hypotheticals can be found throughout the prophetic literature. Key examples include Jer 4:3–4; 6:8; 21:12; Hos 2:4–5; Amos 5:4–6, 14–15; and Mal 3:24.[51]

---

46. Thigpen, *Divine Motive*, 174.

47. Thigpen, *Divine Motive*, 116–17.

48. Thigpen, *Divine Motive*, 121.

49. Sprinkle, "Law and Life," 292.

50. Thigpen, *Divine Motive*, 173.

51. For a discussion of these hypothetical acts of repentance, see Thigpen, *Divine Motive*, 62–63.

So if repentance is not primarily a pathway to salvation, but rather an intention of YHWH to be fulfilled in the new covenant, how do we understand repentance and the monarchy in Kings?[52] Fretheim offers a path forward.

> God *promises* that Israel *will* repent, not least in view of the promises to Abraham (Deut 29:13). The reason is that the Lord is merciful and will not renege on promises made (4:31). That provided a promissory undercurrent in the life of both North (2 Kgs 13:23) and South, enabling a hope beyond exile to be voiced (Deut 4:31) . . . . In effect the articulation of this unconditional promise *enables* Israel's response: human repentance is *possible* only because the divine promise is fully in view.[53]

The book of Kings allows "for good things to happen in response to human actions, including obedience and repentance, but outright cancellation or remission of punishment is not found there," only mitigation of punishment.[54] "This is consistent with the statements on forgiveness in Isaiah, Jeremiah, and Ezekiel, where forgiveness and healing is theocentrically motivated."[55]

In Kings particularly, the theocentric nature of salvation and mitigation is emphasized in the motive statements. In 1 Kgs 8:40–43, Solomon calls on YHWH to save so that he might cause his people to fear him and so that the nations might know him. He implores him to cause the people's captors to have compassion on them, because they are his people and his heritage (1 Kgs 8:51–53). YHWH mitigated the punishment of Solomon because of his past choice of David and his election of Jerusalem as the place where his name would dwell (1 Kgs 11:11–13, 34–36). Again YHWH mitigates the punishment of Abijam, based on his past choice of David and David's faithfulness (1 Kgs 15:4–5).[56] In 1 Kgs 18:37, Elijah appeals to

---

52. For a discussion of the relationship between repentance, salvation, and sanctification, see Fretheim, "Repentance in Former Prophets."

53. Freitheim, "Repentance in Former Prophets," 31–32.

54. Thigpen, *Divine Motive*, 69.

55. Thigpen, *Divine Motive*, 69–70. See esp. Isa 48:9–11; Jer 14:7; Ezek 20:9, 14, 17, 22, 33–39, 44.

56. Here, the restrictive clause רק is applied to David noting his sin with Bathsheba and his murder of Uriah. Although not made explicit here, the motive of "for the sake of David" is part of a cascading motive. David is faithful, but underlying that is the Lord's sovereign choice of David. See 1 Kgs 11:34 for the explicit citation of YHWH's choice in the original context where mitigation is said to be for the sake of David. For a fuller discussion, see Thigpen, *Divine Motive*, 67–68.

YHWH to vindicate him so that the people might know that it was YHWH himself who turned their hearts to repent.[57] In 1 Kgs 20:28, YHWH acts because of the Syrian assertions about his sovereignty and so that people will know him. In 2 Kgs 8:19, YHWH does not yet destroy Judah because of the promises of the Davidic covenant. Jehu's success in bringing Ahab's house to an end did not undo the evil nature of his reign, but he did receive a reward of four generations on the throne in 2 Kgs 10:30. In 2 Kgs 13:4, YHWH is moved by compassion to aid his people in the time of Jehoahaz. The compassion is subsequently qualified as flowing from YHWH's commitment to his covenant with Abraham (2 Kgs 13:23). Similarly, YHWH saves the people in the time of Jeroboam (2 Kgs 14:27). Sennacherib is defeated and sent back to Assyria because of his accusations against YHWH (2 Kgs 19:28), and YHWH specifies that he defends the city of Jerusalem for the sake of David and for his own sake. While informing Hezekiah that his life will be spared for another fifteen years, YHWH again clarifies that his salvation of the city is for the sake of David and for his own sake. The words of judgment found in the book of the Law are upheld, but Josiah escapes having to endure them personally because of his penitent heart (2 Kgs 22:18–20). The force of the punishment is mitigated for Josiah, but the nation is not saved through repentance.

Conclusion

It is time now to unpack the assertion from the introduction that the merciful acts with which YHWH responds to acts of repentance are anticipatory, partial, and pedagogical. Hoyt rightly cautions us against using theologically loaded language like salvation and blessing for the relief from covenant curses and temporal punishments that YHWH brings against his people.[58] Lambert aptly urges interpreters to be more cautious and nuanced with the term repentance. I think both are correct. The question that remains is what is the way forward? Fretheim has suggested that we might consider distinguishing between issues of obedience and disobedience and issues

---

57. House, *1, 2 Kings*, 220.

58. Hoyt, "In Defense," 209. I would suggest that even this statement needs additional attention. It should be asked whether or not salvation and blessing belong together in a single category. Might some aspects of blessing fall in a physical category opposite yet analogous to "deliverance from a physical situation"?

of faith and unbelief. He suggests that in the former prophets "the very relationship with God is at stake," and as such, "radical repentance is the only way into the future." This approach maintains a strong continuity with Deuteronomy, Jeremiah, and Ezekiel where we find that "the tradition is not only to be taught . . . but to be inwardly appropriated" and that this internalization is not the result of repentance, but is rather the act of YHWH that will eventuate in repentance.[59]

Based on this study, I would suggest that we can think broadly about true repentance and other positive responses to YHWH's revelations and actions (such as appeal and petition) as providing occasions for YHWH to respond with what we might think of as anticipatory, partial, and pedagogical acts of forgiveness. This forgiveness is not an ultimate act of salvation. It anticipates the great act of salvation that is announced as part of the new covenant, the forgiveness of sin. It is partial in that it does not fully and completely forgive sin, nor does it effect the heart change described in the prophets. It is pedagogical in that the narrative trajectory of Kings suggests that if YHWH is willing, on the basis of his character, to express mercy even to the wicked kings, then surely his people might rightly hope for mercy and even total forgiveness, even on the other side of the ultimate punishment, exile. To be clear, this is not forgiveness or salvation as traditionally construed theologically. But it is a promissory form of it that leads Israel forward to hope.

Wholehearted and sincere repentance is commanded and expected by YHWH. When repentance, humility, or entreaty are genuine, even if not complete, YHWH responds positively, encouraging his people that he is indeed merciful and forgiving. Yet, without the ability to truly change their heart, repentance in Kings yields, at best, personal reward and mitigation of punishment, an anticipation of full forgiveness that is yet to come. Even in these instances, the underlying motive for YHWH's positive reception of these human acts is his past promises and merciful character. Salvation and the change of heart needed to sustain true repentance and wholehearted obedience and devotion require divine intervention and come only as the result of divine initiative. Repentance flows from these divine acts and is not the ground for salvation in Kings, Jeremiah, and Ezekiel. That YHWH is willing and able to intercede and effect the death-reversing change of heart in his people—so that they might truly repent and follow him

---

59. Fretheim, "Repentance in Former Prophets," 44.

obediently—is the theology of grace to which the books of Kings, Jeremiah, and Ezekiel lead their readers.

7

The Wisdom of Forgiveness

The Case of Job and His Friends

DAVID J. REIMER

Introduction

THE HEBREW BIBLE PROVIDES little for reflection on the dynamics of inter-personal forgiveness—or so it often appears. This very assumption prompts my central research question: what resources does the Hebrew Bible provide for reflecting on the repair of broken human relationships, and how might they inform an ethic of interpersonal forgiveness? Donald Gowan's comprehensive study of forgiveness in the Christian Bible spends vastly more time on divine forgiveness than human. His chapter engaging with the Old Testament, entitled "We Forgive One Another," is only 4 pages long (in a book of 215 pages), which further suggests a paucity of texts relating to forgiveness. But there is something, and that something is Prov 17:9: מכסה־ פשע מבקש אהבה ושנה בדבר מפריד אלוף (One who forgives an affront fosters friendship, but one who dwells on disputes will alienate a friend).[1] Of this verse, Gowan comments: "There is one Old Testament text that commends human forgiveness—probably." This leads to his concluding observation: "So although the Old Testament contains no command to forgive, it is at

---

1. Unless otherwise indicated, English translations are taken from the NRSV.

least commended in the wisdom literature."[2] Even if Gowan's exploration seems overly tentative and restrictive, the pointer to the wisdom literature remains suggestive for addressing the research question posed above.

While the different parts of the Hebrew Bible do not all seem equally promising for this project, one might think that the wisdom traditions would be a sensible place to look for some material that reflects on the nature of human relationships, including their repair after situations of breakdown. Whatever else ancient Near Eastern wisdom is about, the pitfalls and potential at work in human interaction feature regularly. The sages who produced it were keen observers of interpersonal relationships, beginning with the earliest stages of Egyptian instruction literature, running through to the latest phases of early Jewish wisdom literature of the Second Temple period. One of the parade examples of interpersonal forgiveness in the Hebrew Bible is the Joseph story, often taken as part of the wisdom tradition, even if not coming from the books typically seen as comprising the Hebrew Bible's wisdom literature: Job, Proverbs, and Ecclesiastes.[3]

The three wisdom books provide resources of different kinds and quantity of material for reflecting on the repair of broken human relationships. Proverbs has quite a lot to say about the way society works, domestically and politically. But its observations have much more to do with maintaining healthy relationships and avoidance of breakdown than they do with the matter of repair when things go wrong—in spite of Gowan's identification of a key text at 17:9.[4] Ecclesiastes likewise contains instructions bearing on relationships among friends (Eccl 4:11–12), wise dealings in the royal court (8:2–5), and the dangers of anger (7:9), much of which resonates with Proverbs. Here again, however, repair of broken relationships does not come into focus.

Job, by contrast, places this kind of interest in a position of prominence. The dramatic flow of the book of Job is sustained by the encounter of Job with his three friends: Eliphaz, Bildad, and Zophar. Their sympathetic presence quickly sours, however, and the progress of the book is largely a matter of the increasing alienation of Job from his friends, a breakdown that comes early, suddenly, and deteriorates desperately thereafter. By the time the final cycle of speeches is reached, the breach appears to be

2. Gowan, *Bible on Forgiveness*, 89–90.

3. Among others, see McConville, "Forgiveness."

4. My extended study on forgiveness and wisdom deals with these texts; meanwhile, see G. Davies, "Ethics of Friendship."

irreconcilable. The once deferent Eliphaz strikes out at Job, "Is not your wickedness great? There is no end to your iniquities" (22:5). Job, for his part, regards his friends as worse than useless: "I will teach you concerning the hand of God . . . . All of you have seen it yourselves; why then have you become altogether vain?" (הבל תהבלו 27:11–12). But at the book's conclusion, there is an apparent rapprochement between them. The central interest of this essay, then, is to attend to the dynamics of the relationship of Job and his friends, its breakdown, and what contributes to its repair.

Defining Terms

For whatever reason, *forgiveness* has an emotive appeal that *reconciliation* lacks. Unhelpfully, forgiveness also seems to be widely used as an equivalent to reconciliation. This leads to confusion at crucial points. Still, the concepts are deeply intertwined and require also the association of *repentance*. For clarity in this discussion, I understand these related terms this way:

- forgiveness—an injured party setting aside the offense so that it is no barrier to the restoration of relationship with its perpetrator
- repentance—the sorrowful repudiation of an offence that caused hurt by its perpetrator and communicated as such to the one injured
- reconciliation—that healing of a breach in relationship caused by some injury or offense when forgiveness and repentance meet

That is, the double movement of the one offended and the one who caused the offense towards each other, and which results in the healing of that fractured relationship, is captured in these three terms. When either forgiveness or repentance is missing, there can be no reconciliation and no repair of a broken relationship. In modern parlance, forgiveness seems to have taken center stage as the shorthand term for what is really intended by reconciliation, that is, a broken relationship restored.[5]

Job and His Friends

One of the shared features of ANE "righteous sufferer" texts is the social alienation and isolation that the sufferer experiences from his (the

5. The rationale for this account was developed in Reimer, "Apocrypha and Biblical Theology," "Interpersonal Forgiveness," and "Stories of Forgiveness."

protagonists are all male, I believe) normal surroundings.[6] The structure of the book of Job is comprised of a prose prologue and epilogue (chs. 1–2; 42:7–17) that tell the tale of a righteous and wealthy man, deprived of his family, goods, and health (but not his wife) as the outcome of "acts of God" at the prompting of the Satan, which, in the epilogue, are restored to him and more (more goods and new and better children, despite no mention of their mother). In between are extensive poetic dialogues in which Job debates his condition, its causes and likely outcomes, first with "three friends of Job" (שלשת רעי איוב, 2:11), then with Elihu (chs. 32–37), and finally with YHWH (chs. 38:1—42:6).

For my interests, two elements of the book in particular have the potential to contribute to the inquiry about repairing broken human relationships: (1) the programmatic statement about friendship in Job 6:14–23 (possibly issuing out of 6:11–13?) and its echoes through the ensuing cycles of dialogue; and (2) Job's prayer for his three friends in the epilogue (42:7–9), which requires recourse to details of the prologue for illumination. The theme thus runs like a thread through the whole book, although the major speeches by Elihu (chs. 32–37) and YHWH (chs. 38–41) touch on it in only the most tangential ways, if at all.

Job on Betrayal by Friends

After Job's opening soliloquy (ch. 3) in which he despairs of his life in light of the depth of his suffering, Eliphaz responds with gentle counsel, framed around what I regard as the leading question of the dialogues: "Can a mortal be righteous before God? Can a man be pure before his maker?" (4:17). In spite of the deferential tone, the implication remains only thinly veiled: Job must have abandoned the ways of God, and so reproof and chastening (5:17) are what he is due.

As Job's response begins, he still has taken no notice of his friends. But in this speech, Job turns first to address his friends (ch. 6) and then to address God (ch. 7), both for the first time and both premised on statements framed in the third person that Job's deep suffering comes at God's hand (6:2–13) and has irreparably blighted his life (7:1–8). This sets the stage

---

6. Column 1 of the Babylonian text "I will praise the Lord of wisdom" is probably the best-known example: conveniently, *CoS* 1:487–88 (§ 1.153); cf. Annus and Lenzi, *Ludlul bēl nēmeqi.*

for Job's embittered and direct protest to God, the first time Job directly addresses the deity in the second person (7:11–21).

Job's protest to his friends is embedded within this opening salvo. It contains a programmatic statement on the nature of friendship (6:14), framed in difficult Hebrew, which initiates a reflection on this observation, expressed in the third person, and employing evocative figurative language. In v. 21, Job for the first time addresses his friends directly, in order to apply this figure—somewhat harshly—to them, although this verse, too, has a textual problem. In any event, 6:14 remains significant and is important for the structure and progress of Job's thought. Unfortunately, the meaning of the Hebrew in this verse is obscure. Thus S. R. Driver's pithy comment: "Hard and uncertain"![7] So what is the problem—or, better, what are the problems?

A woodenly literal gloss of the MT as it stands goes something like this:

6:14a:	למס	מרעהו	חסד
	To the despairing one (?)	from his friends	—kindness
6:14b:	ויראת	שדי	יעזוב
	and (?) the fear of	the Almighty	he abandons.

The overarching problem is the logical relationship between v. 14a and 14b, and this turns to some extent on where we find the antecedent for the subject of the third person verb ("he abandons") in 14b: who is "he"? The first part of the verse envisages an individual and his friend, but lack of an explicit verb leaves obscure the nature of their relationship around the term חסד. One of these two is doing the abandoning in 14b, but which one? Uncertainty is compounded by two subsidiary linguistic issues: (1) how should למס be understood; and (2) what is the force of the ו conjunction that begins 14b?

(1) The troublesome first word of the verse is typically understood as the *lamed* prefixed preposition with מס, a *hapax legomenon*, from the root מסס (dissolve, melt), so figuratively, "faint, grow fearful."[8] This is reflected early in the English translation tradition, with the AV providing: "To him

---

7. Driver and Gray, *Critical and Exegetical Commentary*, 2:39.
8. *HALOT* 1:606–7; cf. BDB 587.

that is afflicted," with the marginal note, "Hebr. to him that melteth." However, since מם with a *qamets* is a *hapax*, there have long been suggestions for emending the text. The most appealing of these is based on a reading found in Hebrew manuscripts that include an ʾ*aleph*: למאס,[9] the *lamed* with the verb "refuse, withhold" that may lie behind some versional evidence on which some public English translations are based.[10] This is sometimes emended by commentators to read לא מאס, the effect of which is to read "a friend does not refuse חסד."[11]

2) What, then, is the force of the conjunction that begins 14b? The clause that follows in this part of the verse is clear in itself: "he abandons the fear of YHWH." The problem is that, on most readings of 14a, a simple "and" does not yield satisfactory sense. The fitting nuance depends on decisions made regarding the sense of the first part of the verse. If 14a is thought to have something to do with sympathy being given to sufferers, then some kind of concessive term is used, e.g., "although" or the like. Against this, it is sometimes claimed that the *waw* conjunction does not carry a concessive force,[12] although this claim needs a closer look. On the other hand, 14b might be thought of as an *outcome* of 14a, in which case the conjunction reads most naturally as an adversative, "but." If the emendation based on the versions is adopted, the the negative force in the first part carries over to the second part, so the conjunction simply joins two commensurate clauses, "nor." Or, on this same reading, the conjunction is simply ignored and the two clauses are elided.

Altogether, this linguistic and textual scenario gives rise to significantly diverse renderings. For example (each of these having multiple variations):

- AV: "To him that is afflicted, pitie *should be shewed* from his friend; But he forsaketh the feare of the Almighty."

- NJPS: "A friend owes loyalty to one who fails, Though he forsakes the fear of the Almighty . . ."

---

9. *BHS ad loc*, n. b, "למאס mlt mss." See De Rossi, *Variae lectiones*, 4:106, for the list of manuscripts with this reading; the LXX also offers support.

10. E.g., the RSV (and its derivatives with small variations), citing Syriac and Vulgate, with reference to the Targum: "He who withholds kindness from a friend forsakes the fear of the Almighty." On the versions, cf. Dhorme, *Commentary*, 84 (= *Livre de Job*, 77).

11. Gerleman's note a-a in *BHS ad loc*.

12. E.g., Driver and Gray, *Critical and Exegetical Commentary*, 2:40.

- NJB: "Refuse faithful love to your neighbour and you forsake the fear of Shaddai."

- RSV: "He who withholds kindness from a friend forsakes the fear of the Almighty."

Clearly, then, a difficult verse! On balance, however, three considerations should guide the decision taken on the meaning of v. 14: (1) It is clear from what follows that Job regards his friends as unreliable and destructive. This informs the most widely adopted sense in modern versions, that failure to support a "friend in need" is tantamount to apostasy. (2) It is most natural to read with the same subject in both clauses, so that the antecedent for יעזוב (he abandons) is the מס in the previous clause. Taken as it stands, the figurative sense is perfectly adequate in context ("the one who despairs" or the like). (3) In the wider context of ch. 7, as this speech of Job continues, it is clear that—at this point—Job is willing to indulge in a sort of *irrealis* argument. Addressing God, Job exclaims: "If I sin, what do I do to you, you watcher of humanity?" (7:20).[13] It is consistent, then, to see Job adopting this same ploy ("even if") as he turns to, and turns on, his friends in 6:14.

With these considerations in mind, then, the most plausible understanding of this verse sees in it the reasonable expectation a sufferer might have in being the recipient of חסד from friends, even if that suffering might have been occasioned by the apostasy of the sufferer. This takes the *hapax* as a lexeme derived from the root מסס, used figuratively. Clearly, this depends on assigning a concessive force to the *waw* conjunction of 14b, but Driver and Gray were overscrupulous here.[14] The translation in the NET Bible catches this nicely: "To the one in despair, kindness should come from his friend / even if he forsakes the fear of the Almighty."[15]

---

13. Without explicit אם or לֹּ, but on this form of conditional clause: "Any two clauses, the first of which states a real or hypothetical condition, and the second of which states a real or hypothetical consequence thereof, may be taken as a conditional sentence. . . . Conditional sentences in Hebrew may be virtually unmarked" (Lambdin, *Introduction to Biblical Hebrew*, 276). Cf. Joüon and Muraoka, *Grammar of Biblical Hebrew*, §167a; GKC §159h; on Job 7:20 in particular, see Clines, *Job 1–20*, 193–94.

14. Both Joüon and Muraoka, and Arnold and Choi, provide examples of syndetic "concessive" clauses: Joüon and Muraoka, *Grammar of Biblical Hebrew*, §171f; Arnold and Choi, *Guide to Biblical Hebrew*, §5.2.12.

15. This is quite close to Marvin Pope's rendering: "A sick man should have loyalty from his friend, Though he forsake fear of Shaddai," but does not rely on Pope's appeal to the Aramaic to resolve the conundrum of the *hapax* (Pope, *Job*, 52–53).

It is on this basis that Job proceeds to describe his experience of his friends' comfort (Job 2:11) as that of betrayal and treachery (בגדו, 6:15a). The metaphorical language Job uses to describe this experience might at first seem confusing. Verses 15–17 use the figure of the seasonal wadi, in which waters flow only with irregularity and so display dramatically different conditions, in contrast to the "perpetual streams" (Deut 21:4; Amos 5:24) that provide a dependable source of water. But vv. 18–20 shift the image, to focus now on those looking for water, caravaneers in need of relief who go in search of flowing streams but "perish" (v. 18).

The protest launched in v. 14 continues now in vv. 22–23. Even if Job had been guilty of some sin, true friends would have shown חסד (v. 14), but in fact, Job has asked for nothing from them, either to cheat or to deliver. Even in Eliphaz's tentative—at least in comparison with the more brutal iterations that follow—opening speech, Job has heard clearly implied that he has departed from his life of integrity. Thus an irony follows in vv. 24–27: through Eliphaz, the friends have begun to offer their help in the form of "rebuke" (vv. 25–26). According to Prov 9:8, a "wise" person will respond with gratitude, even affection, to such moral guidance. Job, however, is deeply wounded, because the reproof does not accord with the reality of his life: presumably, he experiences Eliphaz's words as שקר, along the lines rather of Prov 25:18, "Like a war club, a sword, or a sharp arrow / is one who bears false witness [שקר] against a neighbor." This inclination of the friends to judge Job's suffering on the basis of their own bespoke narrative of his character goes to the heart of what Robert Davidson calls their "rewriting" of Job's life.[16]

The relationship between Job and his friends, broken down decisively at their first spoken encounter, does not remain static, as Davidson's evocative term indicates. Its movement may be traced, at least in part, by connecting the direct second person plural references Job uses in his speeches. These are less frequent than one might suppose, although he is in constant debate with his friends in chs. 6 to 27.[17] Job speaks in three directions: in the third person, simply to the air, as in his soliloquy of ch. 3, and at the beginning of ch. 6; he addresses his friends, collectively, in the second person plural; and from 7:12, he will often address God directly with the second person singular. Plural addresses cluster at various points, first of all in

---

16. Davidson, *Courage to Doubt*, 169–83, esp. 177.

17. The hymn on wisdom in Job 28 is a poetic interlude; Job's closing speech in chs. 29–31 is a soliloquy and counterpart to his opening speech in ch. 3.

6:21–27 (as discussed above), notably in Job's concluding speech in the first cycle (chs. 12 and 13, the latter of which has the highest density of second masculine plural forms in the book), in response to Elihu (as in ch. 6), again in ch. 16 (with a brief, pointed reprise in 17:10), and then frequently in both chs. 19 (responding to Bildad) and 21 (responding to Zophar).

Job's attention to his friends, collectively, in the summation speech to the first cycle (12:1–6) may be seen as an escalation of his programmatic reflection on friendship towards the suffering in ch. 6. "For the first time in the book, Job is contemptuous of his friends."[18] The reason for this, however, is not so much the accusation of their "laying exclusive claim to wisdom," as Clines suggests (although Job does level this accusation)—the roots of the contempt lie rather in mirroring the contempt he experiences from his friends at their accusations of his alleged moral failure. This is the import of Job's claim to be a "laughingstock" in 12:4, the term שְׂחוֹק used here, as it is in Jer 20:7 and Lam 3:14, of derisive laughter in the face of pain.[19] This opening salvo sets up the longest sustained direct address to the friends in the book in 13:1–17, with this rhetorical phase following through to v. 19.[20] The focus of Job's attention here is the staunch defense of the veracity of his case before God—picking up some legal language from ch. 9—in spite of his friends' lies and if only he could gain a hearing before God. The friends' piety has distorted their perception of Job and impelled them to utter falsehoods (vv. 4, 7–9); Job's hope lies in his integrity before God (vv. 16, 18).

The next node of direct address to the friends by Job comes in the opening verses of ch. 16 (vv. 2–5), and the chapter ends with one of Job's occasional direct mentions of friendship (v. 20). Job's initial rebuke to the friends speaks to their failure to "comfort" (2:11) him: they are, rather "miserable comforters" (מנחמי עמל). He goes on to construct a hypothetical account in which he depicts what his own response would be if the tables were turned, "if you were in my place" (16:4a). The passage can be slightly confusing, as the juxtaposition of vv. 4b and 5 seems rough. I take it that Job is acknowledging that although he could speak words as brusque and hostile as theirs (v. 4b), he would instead bring words of healing and solace

18. Clines, *Job 1–20*, 288.

19. This itself provides an ironic twist on Bildad's optimistic forecast for Job in terms of "laughter" (שְׂחוֹק) in 8:21.

20. The structure of this sprawling speech is variously analyzed and the welter of arrangements outlined and discussed by Clines, who along with a number of other commentators discerns a break after v. 19 (*Job 1–20*, 286–87).

(v. 5; and as he once did, 29:25).[21] This tallies well, then, with his programmatic statement at 6:14. Job's extended and graphic account of his divinely
induced suffering leads to one of his "mediator" statements in 16:19 where
he expresses confidence in a "witness in heaven," perhaps such a mediator
as he longed for in 9:33. The point of interest here is the way in which the
testimony of this "witness" is aligned with friendship in 16:20.[22] Whatever
the (contested) identity of the witness, it is clear that taking up Job's claims
in the heavenly tribunal is what one does for a "neighbor" (6:21)—and what
the three friends before him have failed to do, but rather have opposed him.[23]

The final two clusters of Job's direct address to the friends share features with the preceding texts and deepen the antagonism between them.
In 19:2–6, Job heightens the rhetorical impasse, emphatically rejecting the
friends' account of his moral standing before God and acknowledging his
plight as one with its source in that same God. He excoriates their falsehoods (19:3) and claims the gulf between them has deepened through their
debates (19:5). A remarkable passage piling up detail of his social isolation
(19:13–19) has as its climax the revulsion his friends feel toward him.[24] In
a tone evoking more pathos than rage, he pleads for mercy from "you, my
friends" (19:21).[25] This sets up the famous "redeemer" passage (19:25), in
another resonance with the "witness" of 16:19. Intersecting with his casti-
gation of his friends, Job at the same time hopes against hope that media-
tion of some kind will lead to a declaration of his innocence and release
from his persecution.

The final cluster of second person plural address frames ch. 21, coming
at the conclusion of the second cycle of speeches.[26] The reversals that Job
had previously imagined now take on sharper contours as he displays his

21. So too Clines, *Job 1–20*, 367; cf. Habel, *Book of Job*, 271.

22. With *BHS* n. a-a *ad loc*, I read the first two words as מְלִיצִי רֵעָי, "my intercessor," so
too NIV, NET; with support from Targum, Peshitta, Vulgate, so Dhorme, *Commentary*,
240; also Barth, "לִיץ," 7:551; Gross, "Notes on the Meaning," 238.

23. So Eliphaz in the preceding 15:4–6, 16, with a vivid portrayal of the "wicked" in
vv. 17–35, intended also as a depiction of Job.

24. Not using the familiar רעה but rather מתי סוד, "intimate companions" or the like.

25. The Hebrew of 19:21a is evocative: חנני חנני אתם רעי. "For the moment all thought
of argument is abandoned; he no longer seeks to convince them, or asks them to be just
to him; he asks them to be *kind*" (Driver and Gray, *Critical and Exegtical Commentary*,
1:169; emphasis original).

26. It is possible that 31:29–34 could also be added to this small corpus, although
here Job's reflections remain more abstract and are not directed specifically to his three
friends.

suffering to his friends and instructs them in the "consolation" (21:2) they ought to offer him. It amounts to a renewed call for their silence, if they cannot speak words of genuine comfort (21:5). Like ch. 19, direct address picks up again later in the passage (21:27–29, 34). Here Job's tone turns more accusatory, as his understanding of their hostility implies an element of premeditation, which also has some resonance with the extended travel metaphor for friendship that provided the substance of Job's reflection in ch. 6. Verse 34, the final statement to conclude the second cycle, states the matter starkly: "How then will you comfort me with empty nothings [הבל]? There is nothing left of your answers but falsehood [מעל]."

In the progression of these five passages that trace the ever-deepening rift between Job and his friends, it might be too schematic to see something like the phases of grief that typically accompany loss: the isolation of ch. 6; the intensifying anger of chs. 12–13; an element of bargaining in the thought experiment in reciprocity in ch. 16; depression in the deep social alienation of ch. 19; culminating not in "acceptance" or acquiescence but with Job's renewed commitment to the veracity of his claim, despite his broken state, in ch. 21.[27] Graham Davies, attending to a different set of textual cues, sees Job objecting to his friends' behavior on four levels: their "mercenary attitude" (6:27; 17:5); their "mockery" (12:4; 16:20); their "abandonment" of him (19:13–19; cf. 30:29); and their "pitiless attitude" (19:21).[28]

In stark terms, then, this reflection on broken friendship is just the opposite of what my project is interested in: how to *repair* broken relationships. However, it does not take much imagination to see how reflecting more deeply on Job's treatment of the theme here informs the project of repair as well. Job looks minimally for חסד from those to whom he looks as friends (as "brothers," 6:14–15), but beyond that, he demands a response from them based on the evidence of their knowledge of his life of integrity, not on the depth of his suffering. The intervention of Elihu forestalls the intervention of YHWH, but that unexpected and dramatic encounter sets up a dénouement in the epilogue that is likewise unexpected: the renewed fellowship of Job and his friends.

27. These, of course, parallel the famous stages associated with the work of Elisabeth Kübler-Ross. Although it has fallen into disfavor in some quarters (e.g., Corr, "Should We Incorporate"), the account persists in holding out some explanatory power for the variety of experience of grieving.

28. G. Davies, "Ethics of Friendship," 142–43. Both accounts have some reflex in Job's concluding soliloquy in chs. 29–31, which review his past life, present condition, and future prospects, anticipating the affirmation of his moral standing.

Job's Prayer for His Friends

The prologue and epilogue of Job sometimes get short shrift, and can be undervalued in analyses of the book, but together they offer a significant insight into our investigation into repairing broken human relationships.[29] The focal point for this comes in Job's two episodes as sacrificial intercessor. The only two verses in Job to use the *hiphil* of עלה are 1:5 and 42:8—the only verses to mention sacrifice at all, in fact. Norman Habel is keen to point out the interrelationship between these two episodes.[30] The "proleptic" sacrifice of 1:5 anticipates the offerings made in the final chapter, while at the same time providing an ironic foil to Job's regularly articulated sense that he lacks any mediator to perform this function on his behalf.

Job's devoted vigilance in 1:4–5 is worth a moment's reflection. The Hebrew Bible has no prescriptions for "what-if" sacrifices—something different from the instructions of Lev 4 for dealing with the sins of ignorance that come to light. While Job's piety has been variously evaluated,[31] the frame it provides for the book as a whole remains clear. It is likely, then, that this initial occurrence alerts us to the contours of its counterpart in ch. 42. As Hoffman notes, this episode at least plants in the reader's mind—and, within the narrative world of the text, in that of the character of Job as well—the real possibility of some deleterious and impious behavior on the part of Job's sons. So when their sudden and tragic deaths occur, Job can only assume that either his intercession and sacrifices failed in expiating their guilt or that YHWH smote them in their innocence.

Such are the conclusions Job might have drawn as he reflected on the value of his sacrificial prayers. In the epilogue, Job is called upon to intercede on behalf of those he regards as betrayers of his trust and who have spent the bulk of their share of the dialogues in unjust and embittered accusations of the one now to be their intercessor. How will Job regard this task he is now being given?

---

29. For what follows, cf. Clines, "Seven Interesting Things"; also Cooper, "'Reading and Misreading."

30. Habel, *Book of Job*, 87–88.

31. See the brief comments on this circumstance in Brenner, "Job the Pious?," 43–44; and Hoffman, "Relation," 167–68. Brenner is suspicious of Job's hyper-religious activity and regards it almost as a parody; Hoffman demonstrates that the sons' behavior and Job's ritual actions bear an intrinsic connection to the moral possibilities raised in the dialogues.

But putting it this way still slightly misstates the scenario, and we must attend to the narrator's assignment of speech and recipient in these texts. What YHWH says to Job appears in chs. 38–41, and this elicits Job's reply in 42:1–6. As Clines observes (and others have before him),[32] nothing in that extended speech from the whirlwind illuminates Job concerning his own life and the strange and incommensurate circumstances in which he suffers. It has been entirely directed to asserting the nature of God's power (which Job knew all too well; cf. 9:2–20), and governance of the created order (on which Job was a little shaky, his understanding being deepened by this speech). Notably, it is to Eliphaz that YHWH gives the instruction through whom to seek prayer and offer sacrifice (42:7–8)—and this they do (v. 9). Both the request and its fulfilment should surprise the reader. Eliphaz knows, and readers of this book of Job know, that YHWH has sided with Job, declared his innocence, affirmed the veracity of his speech, and condemned the friends for their culpable folly. But does Job know? How does he regard the substantial, even extravagant, sacrifice required (42:8)?[33] It all depends on what Eliphaz has told him (if we follow Clines's sense of the narrative here, that the instructions YHWH gives to Eliphaz are not overheard by Job). However we solve that conundrum, the story is clear that Job's prayer is "accepted" (וישׂא יהוה את־פני איוב, 42:9b).

Readers' attention throughout the centuries has been fixed on the divine-human axis in these interactions.[34] This largely grows out of the sense that if the book of Job is about anything, it must be about unmerited suffering and the possibility of cosmic justice. That is fair enough. But it is also the case that the epilogue of Job is about Job's social world being put right. Thus far in the book, he has been bereaved of his children, had a fundamental disagreement with his wife (ch. 2), engaged in an increasingly fractious and ill-tempered debate with three friends (chs. 3–31), suffered the rebukes and instruction of the younger Elihu (chs. 32–37), and listened—mostly in silence—to a divine disquisition on the ordering of the universe. Job's social world has wholly collapsed. Now all this is about to be put to rights, but it involves the resetting of interpersonal relationships. This is not likely to be easy. Regarding the

32. Clines, "Seven Interesting Things," 13–14.

33. Clines, "Seven Interesting Things," 15, associates the grand sacrifice with the intensity of the indignation YHWH feels towards the friends, since YHWH indicates that, without the sacrifice, he will treat them נבלה (there is no "according to," etc.).

34. For a critique of the dominant perspective with attention to traditional interpretation see (among many others) Cooper, "Sense of the Book."

requirement placed on Eliphaz of approaching Job to intercede, David Clines observes the personal dynamics at stake:

> Only a supplication from his "servant" Job, who says all the right things about him, will suffice to hold him back from the improper behavior he contemplates. But why should Yahweh suppose that Job will be willing to pray for his so-called friends? What does Job owe them, that he should plead with God on their behalf? Is God counting on Job to resurrect his old loyalty toward his friends? Are some residual bonds between Job and the friends all that stand between them and God's anger? Or does he expect that at the end of the day, when there is conflict between the divine realm and the human, humans will stick together? Yahweh seems to be expecting more of Job than he has a right to.[35]

The translation of 42:10 adds to our impressions of the transaction being enacted here.[36] English translations typically imply that Job's restoration takes place at some point subsequent to his intercession for his friends, as in the NRSV's "when he had prayed for his friends." However, the Hebrew construction at this point is an infinitive construct with a (subject) suffix, prefixed with בְּ-, used to convey "the correspondence of two actions in time."[37] And thus it is here (בהתפללו), so that the preferred rendering would be "And the LORD restored the fortunes of Job *while he prayed* for his friends."[38] Whatever it might overtly or practically mean for Job's fortunes to be restored at this moment—since there can be no children, flocks, etc.—we can take it that his standing before YHWH and his friends has been repaired.

One further aspect of this small scene deserves attention. Job's intercession not only reestablishes the interpersonal relationship among this

---

35. Clines, "Coming to Theological Conclusion," 219.

36. Clines, "Seven Interesting Things," 16–17.

37. On the preposition בְּ- with the infinitive for temporal simultaneity, cf. Joüon and Muraoka, *Grammar of Biblical Hebrew*, §166l.

38. This feature is rarely remarked on by commentators but is apparently registered by Karl Budde: "בהתפללו וגו lässt auch bei rein zeitlicher Auffassung den ursächlichen Zshg. zwischen Fürbitte und Heilung ausser jedem Zweifel" (*Buch Hiob*, 255). Franz Delitzsch similarly calls attention to the narrative sequence here: "The moment in which Job prayed for his friends became, as the climax of a life that is well-pleasing to God, the turning point of glory to him. The Talmud has borrowed from here the true proverb: כל המתפלל בעד חברו נענה תחלה, i.e. he who prays for his fellow-men always finds acceptance for himself first of all" (*Biblical Commentary*, 2:388; the source for the saying appears to be *Bava Qamma* 92a).

small social grouping, it also reestablishes "normal" communications between YHWH and Job. While Balentine's speculations on the content of Job's prayer—left unstated by our Joban author—as being a prayer *for* God, somehow enabling God to fulfil his true identity, may not finally persuade,[39] Balentine's reading alerts us to the way in which this prayer reverses the flow of Job's first halting words of recognition in 40:3–5 when he renounces further speech, only partially undone in the "confession" of 42:2–6, enigmatic as it is. Here, while Job's own words are not reported, the ensuing narrative confirms that his speaking with God on behalf of his friends has had its proper effect. But Balentine is surely right to conclude that the text "leads us to think that the *friends' relationship with God* is different after Job prays. The text also daringly invites us to think that, after Job prays, *God's relationship with the friends* is different."[40]

While much remains between the lines, the only satisfactory unpacking of the terse narrative detail that frames the story is that the triangular relationship between YHWH, Job, and his friends (and later, his estranged family, 42:11), which had been so distorted through the calamities of the prologue and the calumnies of the dialogues, has been healed. Eliphaz, with or on behalf of his friends, has articulated God's decision; Job has provided the sacrificial intercession his treacherous friends request (as he had once done for his own family); YHWH restores שלום. We might even see it as a worked example or case study for Prov 16:7—"When the ways of people please the LORD, he causes even their enemies to be at peace with them." Well has Graham Davies suggested that the book of Job deserves study as "a dispute about the nature of true friendship."[41]

---

39. Balentine, "My Servant Job," 503. His observation (with Brenner, 507–8) that 42:7's "After the LORD had spoken these words"—which conclude a speech by Job (!)— further give the sense that the "natural" communications (or at least, the order that prevailed as the book opens) have not yet been restored.

40. Balentine, "My Servant Job," 514; emphasis original. With reference to the first of those claims, Balentine cites Testament of Job 42:8: "And I took them [the friends' sacrifices] and made an offering on their behalf, and the Lord received it favorably and forgave their sin."

41. G. Davies, "Ethics of Friendship," 143.

Conclusion

There is a modern proverb attributed to Benjamin Franklin—"An ounce of prevention is worth a pound of cure."[42]

Wisdom literature does not, as a rule, contemplate changing things. It is, rather, concerned to describe how the world works and then to situate human behavior within it—ultimately (and theologically) with a view to living in accord with the structures that God has ordained for creation. As such, it should not be a surprise if there is little attention given to fixing broken things (i.e., effecting change), whether that is in the sphere of interpersonal or domestic or social relationships, and whether these be casual or official.

Even if the preponderance of attention is given to maintenance and prevention, the book of Job, at any rate, provides suggestive resources for perceiving and then performing those actions that lead to the healing of broken relationships, as the victims set aside the offense as an impediment to renewed relationship, as offenders recognize and repudiate the injurious acts, and through which YHWH reweaves the fabric of a peaceful society.

One further feature of this dynamic of reconciliation requires comment. It is the intervention of YHWH that precipitates the chain of events leading to the rapprochement of Eliphaz, Bildad, and Zophar with Job. Job's encounter with God—long hoped for, but never expected—radically modifies his perception of divine governance and his own place in the cosmic order. The humbling admonition, correction, and instruction Eliphaz receives from YHWH is much more brief than Job's extended encounter but brings an equally dramatic inversion of the friends' theological assumptions and ethical corollaries, which would in turn demand approaching Job (Job!) to assuage the divine wrath directed against them.

Tracing the dynamic of the breaking and healing of the relationship between Job and his friends cannot, then, neglect this theological dimension. At least on this account, reconciliation is not simply a human achievement. When it comes to interpersonal forgiveness, repentance, and reconciliation, then, the shared perspective of wisdom literature remains apposite, and the fear of the Lord truly is the beginning of wisdom, even for the repair of human relationships.[43]

---

42. Franklin, "On Protection of Towns."

43. Proverbs 1:7; cf. Job 28:28; Eccl 8:12.

8

The Forgiveness of Others
in the Old Testament

J. Gordon McConville

The Forgiveness of Others in the New Testament

My question is how far the forgiveness of others is exemplified and valued in the Old Testament, and to what end. At the outset, it is important to note how central it is in the New Testament, especially in the teaching of Jesus. In the Lord's Prayer, Jesus teaches his disciples to pray for God's forgiveness "as we also have forgiven our debtors" (Matt 6:12). This is echoed in his other teaching, for example, in the parable in Matt 18:21–25 in which a servant, released from a large debt by his master, responds not by imitating the generosity shown to him but by exacting a smaller debt from a fellow-servant (Matt 18:21–35). This is told in answer to Peter's famous question as to how often he should forgive another[1] who repeatedly sins against him (18:21). Forgiveness of others is clearly an imperative in the Gospel accounts of Jesus's teaching.

---

1. Peter says "my brother" (*ho adelphos mou*).

Jesus's teaching on forgiveness of others as a proper response to God's forgiveness has a precedent in the Apocryphal book of Sirach, at 27:30—28:7. "Forgive your neighbor the wrong he has done you, and then your sins will be pardoned when you pray" (28:2, NRSV). The passage goes on to reflect on the destructiveness of harbored anger, a point to which we shall return below.

Yet this kind of reflection on the forgiveness of others is by no means prominent in the Old Testament. Hence the inquiry that follows.

Only God Can Forgive Sins?

In response to Jesus's pronouncement of forgiveness to a man he has healed, some scribes object: "Who can forgive sins but God alone?" (Mark 2:7). Their point is not directly about human forgiveness of others but concerns God's authority to forgive sins in general, which Jesus seems to them to be usurping. Even so, it is a useful starting-point for a consideration of forgiveness in the Old Testament. Is there a connection there between divine and human forgiveness?

A search on the leading words translated "forgive" in the Old Testament shows that the subject of forgiveness is overwhelmingly God. The verb סלח only ever has God as subject. It is frequent in priestly, or atonement, texts. In a typical example, in Lev 5:1–10, a number of situations are addressed in which a person may become guilty, the person brings a guilt-offering, atonement is made by the priest ([עליו] וכפר), and the person is forgiven (ונסלח לו, 5:10). The formula occurs nine times (with guilt-offerings and sin-offerings) in Lev 4–5,[2] and also in Lev 19:22; Num 15:25–28). These texts embrace both holiness offences, which make one ritually unclean (as in 5:1–10), and offences committed in the social sphere, as in 6:2–7. All such have to be atoned for and forgiven. Common to them is the need to put right a disruption in the order of things, so that life may continue.

If we look for some underlying concepts in this sphere of the religious life of Israel, one important idea is that of restitution. In Lev 5:16, the offence evidently has a money value, which comes to the sanctuary and the priest by way of compensation. That which has been "done amiss" (RSV, חטא) in respect of the "holy thing" (הקדש), the offerer must make good (ישלם), according to a valuation not spelt out in the text, and add a fifth to it, as well as the sacrifice of a ram.

---

2. Leviticus 4:20, 26, 31, 35; 5:10, 13, 16, 18, 26.

In Num 5:7–8, the offence in question is not only against God but also against another person. Here, too, full compensation must be made to the offended party, plus a fifth of the value, together with the sacrifice. In a different expression, the offerer "turns back" his אשם upon his (own) head[3] and gives it to the one to whom he did the wrong (Num 5:7).[4] The אשם is therefore the guilt, the deficiency that is caused by it,[5] and the compensation made for it. This text is especially revealing, because the restitution must be made even though the offended party is no longer present; that is, the deficiency is an objective fact that goes beyond the interpersonal relationship.[6]

In these atonement texts, therefore, that which is forgiven is seen as a deficiency, which has somehow to be compensated for. The deficiency is not limited to the hurt done to another human being but exists in an order of things in which God and human society have their part.

The forgiveness of God (סלח) occurs also in non-atonement texts, that is, where God is simply said (or asked) to forgive the sin of Israel, often through intercessory prayer. Thus Moses prays for God to forgive Israel following the sin of the golden calf (Exod 34:9). Solomon prays for forgiveness repeatedly[7] at the dedication of the newly built temple in 1 Kgs 8:27–53, predicated on future instances of sin and repentance. Amos pleads for forgiveness of the people when the Lord has revealed to him his purpose to punish them (Amos 7:2). In Jeremiah, God declares that he will forgive Israel as a function of the new covenant he will make with them, when the *torah* will be "written on their hearts" (Jer 31:34; 33:8; cf. 50:20), and in other cases in Jeremiah, forgiveness is God's response to Israel repenting of its sins (Jer 5:1, 7; 36:3; cf. Isa 55:7). Psalmists pray for forgiveness or invoke it as an attribute of God (Ps 25:11; 86:5; 103:3). Daniel, as intercessor, does likewise (Dan 9:9, 19). And the lamenter in Lamentations complains that the Lord has *not* forgiven (Lam 3:42).

We might term these cases *prophetic*. It is interesting, on the face of it, that סלח forgiveness is not confined to the holiness procedures. (In some

3. ‏והשיב את־אשמו בראשו.

4. ‏ונתן לאשר אשם לו.

5. The basic idea of אשם as "deficiency" is illustrated in Joel 1:18: ‏עדרי הצאן נאשמו (there is no pasture for the flocks).

6. For the verb שלם as "make restitution" in cases of civil wrongs, see Exod 21:37 (EVV36); and fourteen times in ch. 22, including the double expression ‏ישלם שלם in vv. 2, 5, 13 (1, 4, 12).

7. 1 Kings 8:30, 34, 36, 39, 50. There are three further instances in Kings: 2 Kgs 5:18 (2x), 24:4, in relation to Naaman and Manasseh respectively.

cases, the worshipper is or may be making sacrifices even while praying.) Importantly, prayer plays a part in both kinds of case.

In these prophetic texts, the outcome is also that life is enabled to continue because of God's willingness to forgive. However, in these cases, we have entered the sphere of the divine governance of the world. This forgiveness does not rule out the possibility of punishment for sin (Num 14:18–25; cf. Isa 40:1–2). Forgiveness and continuing life may be contingent either on prayer and repentance or simply on God's grace, which requires no compensation. Forgiveness belongs in the sphere of God's judgment and providence, and so in the arguably unresolved tension between repentance and grace as conditions of the divine favor.

The picture is only slightly different when we look at the other leading term for forgiveness, namely נשא, "lift, take away." In its general use, it has God as subject and can be in parallel with סלח, as in Exod 34:7–9 and Num 14:18–19. In these texts, forgiving iniquity is not just an action but a characteristic of God, as also in Ps 99:8. Yet here, too, there is the possibility of God not forgiving, or "not clearing" the guilty (ונקה לא ינקה [Exod 34:7]). The possibility of non-forgiveness is presumed in other texts. Isaiah prays that God would *not* pardon idolaters (Isa 2:9). Job asks why God does not pardon his iniquity (Job 7:21). Judgment and forgiveness lie within the providence of God, and are played out together in the Old Testament's underlying narrative, notably in the prophets (Isa 40:1–2; cf. Isa 33:24; Hos 14:3 [EVV 2]).

In some of these texts, human actors are involved, not only as receiving God's forgiveness (or not) but in engaging with God about it, hence Isaiah's prayer against idolatry (Isa 2:9) and Job's complaint about the way in which justice works in his case (Job 7:21). In some cases where one person asks another for forgiveness, the issue is really whether God will forgive. In Exod 10:17, Pharaoh requests Moses and Aaron to "forgive" (נשא) his sin— by praying to God. In 1 Sam 15:25, Saul begs Samuel to forgive him (נשא) for he has sinned, and Samuel refuses because "YHWH has rejected him." These cases, therefore, are hardly instances of humans forgiving others. The reference here, too, is to an objective removal of the guilt of sin, rather than a reconciliation between human subjects in itself.

On the basis of the texts we have reviewed so far, we can conclude the following: sin causes a deficiency in the right order of things. God has the prerogative of forgiveness and exercises it in several ways, by his institution of a formal system of reparation in the worship of Israel or simply by his providential decision in the sphere of his ordering the world. This is true even when humans are offended, as in Num 5:7–8 (cf. Ps 51.[8]) Sin damages relationships among God and humans, beyond offences done between humans, because sin is an offence against God and his ordering of the world. Humans engage with God in prayer, that is, in negotiations about justice and forgiveness. God's forgiveness repairs damage done and enables flourishing new life.

Forgiveness and Restoration

If forgiveness lies in the realm of the justice or judgment of God, a connection is suggested between it and certain other concepts concerning the divine ordering of things. One such concept—suggested by the book of Amos—is צדקה (righteousness), which is both a characteristic of God (who is described as צדיק in Deut 32:4; Ps 119:137) and the principle by which God acts in the world.[9] This quality can also be predicated of humans (Noah, Gen 6:9; Abraham, Gen 18:19[10]), and it enters the realm of Israel's judicial life. In Deut 25:1, the innocent party in a lawsuit is pronounced "righteous" or, more suitably to the context, innocent (והצדיקו את־הצדיק). In a telling case, Judah declares of his daughter-in-law Tamar, whom he was on the point of condemning as a prostitute, "she is more righteous than I" (צדקה ממני [Gen 38:26]). Here is an instance of the ethics of the Old Testament, as "imitation of God."[11] And Joseph Jensen uses it as a key to understanding the book of Amos. As God has (implicitly) "treated Israel with צדקה" (since he vindicated them against the more powerful [Amos 2:9–10]), he requires

---

8. Psalm 51, with its superscription, might be included here. When David confesses his sin to God, saying: "Against you, you alone, have I sinned" (Ps 51:6 [EVV v. 4]), the superscription points the reader to his sin with Bathsheba, involving the murder of Uriah, and resulting in the death of her infant son by him. The superscription thus interprets these serious sins against other humans as sins against God.

9. YHWH's "righteousness" (צדק/צדקה) is regularly appealed to by the psalmists as the ground of God's action in the world and of their hope. Ps 119 illustrates this, with thirteen occurrences. Pss 111–12 afford a good example of the expected human reciprocation of God's righteousness (Ps 111:3; 112:3, 4, 6, 9). Righteousness is sometimes portrayed as a characteristic of the created world itself, as in Isa 45:8; cf. Ps 85:11 (EVV v.10).

10. In the paired concept צדקה ומשפט (righteousness and justice).

11. This is one of the categories proposed by John Barton, "Understanding Old Testament Ethics."

the same standard of Israel;[12] they too should "let justice [מִשְׁפָּט] roll down like waters, and righteousness [צְדָקָה] like an ever-flowing stream" (Amos 5:24). מִשְׁפָּט and צְדָקָה form a common pairing in the prophets (and Deuteronomy) and together denote the desire of God for a society that loves and practices justice. If such justice is not practiced, then God will come in judgment. Jensen finds in this principle a correspondence between Amos and the Lord's Prayer, in which Jesus teaches his disciples to pray "forgive us our debts as we forgive our debtors."

In Amos, the course of the divine צְדָקָה occupies the same space as the divine forgiveness. Amos's prayer for forgiveness for Israel is acceded to twice (7:2-3, 4-6) but finally not (7:7—9:8).[13] Should God forgive Israel if Israel is intent on pursuing injustice in its inner relations? The divine צְדָקָה requires a kind of human conduct that looks beyond its narrowly conceived, self-centered interests, in recognition of the higher interest of a common good.

Forgiveness between Human Persons

Person-to-person forgiveness is not absent in the Old Testament, and certain texts postulate it clearly. The theme of forgiveness and reconciliation may be said to lie at the heart of the story of Joseph and his brothers.[14] Joseph's actions towards his brothers are often considered inexplicably harsh. He engages in a long-drawn-out negotiation with them, in which he conceals his identity and suppresses things that are profoundly important to him, especially his longing for reunion with his father. The purpose, apparently, is to create something new in the relationship. The brothers who could not "speak peace" to each other (Gen 37:4) are able finally to converse (45:15).

It may be asked, however, whether Joseph has truly forgiven them. This is the brothers' own question in 50:15-21, in a petition couched obliquely and apprehensively in the form of a command from their father (vv. 16-17). Strictly speaking, we do not know whether Joseph has forgiven them in his heart. But we can observe two factors that play into this culminating scene:

---

12. Jensen, *Ethical Dimensions of Prophets*, 90.

13. I take 9:11-15 to look beyond the immediate crisis in Amos's time.

14. This is argued by White, *Narration and Discourse*, 232-75; G. Fischer, "Josefgeschichte als Modell." Fung agrees but with the qualification that the story highlights the difficulties in the way of reconciliation among brothers (*Victim and Victimizer*, 169).

first, the apparent change in the brothers themselves, and second, Joseph's perspective concerning the divine purpose.

Regarding the first of these, Joseph has shown a keen interest in the brothers' state of mind. In his elaborate and long-drawn-out play on their fears, he has exposed their evil to themselves. The speech of Judah (Gen 44:18–34) is the dramatic turning point because of its authenticity, as Judah recasts the history of the father and brothers in a way that displays penitence and human sympathy. This development was not necessarily engineered by Joseph for his own satisfaction. His true interests are more surely revealed by the emotional collapse of his dissembling upon first making himself known: "I am Joseph: is my father still alive?" (45:3). His manipulation of the brothers, it seems, was subordinate to his purpose to bring about restoration and future possibility.

Regarding the divine purpose, one could read his answer to the brothers' petition for forgiveness (50:15–21) as evasive. But in fact, his response is telling. When he says "Am I in the place of God?," the effect is to direct attention away from his own part in the events and to the greater purpose that God had in them. The evil intention of the brothers is placed in the perspective of that purpose and has even played a part in furthering it. Likewise, Joseph's personal feelings remain in the background. But his actions are crucial to the realization of the divine intention that he perceives.

In the case of Joseph, then, forgiveness consists in refraining from taking revenge or retribution for the sake of a higher good. A further angle on this is afforded by the story of David and Nabal in 1 Sam 25. The setting is the phase of David's history when he is on the run from Saul and, together with a band of men, is moving around remote, wilderness areas of Judah. The episode is bracketed between two narratives of close encounters between David and Saul, in which David spares the life of the king who has become his enemy.[15]

In 1 Sam 24, David refrains from taking Saul's life in spite of his opportunity to secure his own by doing so. David gives two reasons: Saul is "the LORD's anointed" (vv. 7, 11 [EVV 6, 10]), and vengeance for evil is the Lord's (v. 13 [EVV12]). Though he had motives for killing Saul, both for his own safety and as a matter of revenge,[16] he acts instead on factors

---

15. The narrative relationship between the Nabal story and the two accounts of the sparing of Saul has been illuminated by Gordon, "David's Rise."

16. The element of revenge is expressed in the phrase ונקמני יהוה ממך (The LORD will avenge me upon you [v. 13 (EVV12)]).

that transcend his immediate interests. The narrative's commentary on this comes from Saul himself, who is struck to the heart by David's greater virtue, compared with his own murderous intent. David is "more righteous" than he,[17] for he has repaid evil with good (v. 18 [EVV 17]). He has departed from the norm of self-preservation and revenge (v. 20a [EVV 19a]), at potential cost to himself. Because of this, Saul knows that David will indeed be king.

The narrative serves as background to the episode with Nabal and Abigail (ch. 25), which develops the theme of leaving vengeance to the Lord (25:26). Nabal, a rich but boorish sheep farmer, has refused David's request for hospitality, and David resolves to take bloody revenge (vv. 5–13). The situation is saved by the quick action of Nabal's beautiful and intelligent wife Abigail. She not only remedies the failure of Nabal's hospitality but also frames the situation in terms of guilt and forgiveness: "Let the blame [עון][18] be upon me," she pleads (v. 24), and then: "forgive the trespass [שא נא לפשע]"[19] of your maidservant" (v. 28). (The transfer of Nabal's guilt to herself is a device of her persuasive art; but the issue of a wrong done, and its possible consequences, is of the essence.)

Abigail emerges as the interpreter of the unfolding events. She knows that if David keeps himself from the bloodguilt entailed in his proposed slaughter of Nabal's male household, he will enjoy the Lord's favor, and his kingship will indeed be established. Such restraint is the key that will unlock "all the good" the Lord has promised David (v. 30), with an allusion to the promise of a "sure house" (בית נאמן [v. 28]), anticipating the divine promise in 2 Sam 7:13–16. "All the good" (כל . . . את־הטובה [v. 30]) suggests a bountiful and ordered life in the land over which David will be king (cf. והעטב [v. 31]; Deut 6:21–25). David himself will know the special care of the Lord (v. 29), who will protect him and defeat his enemies. And all this he will enjoy in freedom from the shadow of guilt. That this encounter with Abigail has a certain formative effect on David appears in the second episode with Saul, in which David, once again recognizing Saul as "the LORD's anointed," adds to his rationale for not killing him: "who can raise his hand against the LORD's anointed *and be innocent*?" (ונקה 26:9; cf. 24:7,

---

17. צדיק אתה ממני. This is similar to Judah's confession regarding Tamar in Gen 38:26.

18. עון may be both sin and guilt; it is often translated "iniquity."

19. פשע belongs to the Old Testament's extensive vocabulary of sin, often with a nuance of rebellion or "trespass." "Forgive," in this case, is נשא, שא (lift, take away).

11 [EVV 6, 10]). This chimes with Abigail's argument that David should avoid bloodguilt in the case of Nabal (25:26, 33).[20]

At the heart of Abigail's argument, also in 25:26, 33, is that David should refrain from trying to deliver himself by his own hand.[21] The theological home of this trope is the relationship between divine and human action in the furtherance of God's purpose (as in the Joseph story). All the texts that feature a similar usage show that only God can ultimately bring help and safety. In David's restraint, he recognizes that God alone can deliver him from his present danger—and so enable him to exercise his kingship with integrity, free from the destructive encumbrance of bloodguilt. In the context of the books of Samuel, that kingship is entwined with God's purpose to sustain his covenantal relationship with Israel. David therefore subordinates his impulse to secure his own life, and to avenge his insulted honor (cf. 25:39), to his belief in a greater purpose of God for Israel, revived by the wit and rhetoric of Abigail. Again, as with Joseph, that belief does not belie his responsibility to act aright. Indeed, David is God's chosen instrument for the deliverance of Israel (2 Sam 3:18). The episode may be seen, therefore, as aligning David's personal desire with that of God, a moment in the making of "the man after God's own heart" (1 Sam 13:14). His parting instruction to Abigail, "Go up in peace to your house" (v. 35), is a pointer to his awakening sense of his vocation to use power to create harmony, rather than violence to inflame.

---

20. For the formative nature of David's encounter with Abigail, cf. McCarter: "[David] does not exhibit the necessary restraint spontaneously, but *learns* it in the course of events . . . . [He] is like the young man to whom so much of the Book of Proverbs is addressed, who finds himself in contact with the proverbial 'fool' (*nabal* . . .) and the proverbial 'stalwart woman' ('*eshet chayil*; see Prov 31:10)" (*I Samuel*, 401).

21. The phrase והושע ידך לך (v. 26) may be translated "your own hand delivering you." Verse 33 has a slight variation: והשע ידי לי. The phrase means accomplishing victory or deliverance or, in Driver's words, implies "an exploit or success, achieved against opposing obstacles by *force*" (Driver, *Notes on Hebrew Text*, 155; emphasis original). Its closest analogies in the Old Testament all imply or affirm that it is the Lord who gets victory for his people, often against the idea that they might do so themselves; cf. Jdg 7:2; Job 40:14; Ps 98:1; Isa 59:16; 63:5. In the present case, "getting deliverance by one's own hand" is often taken to mean "getting revenge" (KJV, NIV, NRSV). While this has some warrant from the context (24:13 [EVV 12]), it does not catch the sense of the phrase, which is better translated "getting victory for yourself" (Klein, *1 Samuel*, 244; cf. McCarter, *I Samuel*, 401). ESV's "working salvation with my own hand" (v. 33) unjustifiably imports connotations of ישע from other texts. On the syntax of the phrase, Driver notes that the infinitive absolute (השע) following an infinitive construct and followed by a noun that is effectively its subject is rare (*Notes on Hebrew Text*, 155).

The narrative hardly suggests that David has actually forgiven Nabal in his heart; on the contrary, he rejoices in his death, as the judgment of God upon him for his insult to David's honor (25:39).

In both these cases of personal forgiveness, the protagonists' inner attitude is not the essential point. Joseph's emotional engagement is beyond doubt (45:2-3; 50:17), and his case is an intriguing study in the interaction between his actions in his public and official role and his life as an individual.[22] Even so, his innermost feelings towards the brothers remain hidden. The idea of heartfelt forgiveness is even more remote in the case of David, yet the narrative element of personal formation in chs. 24-26 evidently attaches importance to his moral and spiritual condition. In both personalities, therefore, one might discern a relationship between the private character and the public actor.

Both David and Joseph, by their actions, testify to an aspiration beyond their own immediate interests. For Joseph, it is about enabling a reconstitution of his broken family, in the context of a belief in God's sovereign purpose in events; for David, it consists in his recognition that God's ways for Israel have precedence over the narrow horizons of his own concerns. It would be easy to interpret both characters skeptically or reductively. Joseph may aim pragmatically to protect the interests of his father and Benjamin within the family.[23] David may calculate that Abigail has rightly divined his best tactics for smoothing his way to power in Israel. Yet the respective narratives pull against such reductions. Joseph, echoing a theme of Proverbs, knows that God works out his purposes according to a rationality higher than the human and does so for his good purposes (Gen 50:20; cf. Prov 16:9). David's blessing of Abigail for her wise words has the mark of authentic recognition of their truth, and in sending her back to her home "in peace," he has little to gain, since he has no foreknowledge of Nabal's early death or of his acquisition of Abigail as his wife. David no doubt carries his anointing by Samuel as Saul's successor in his memory (1 Sam 16:13), and both Saul and Abigail know the strength of his claim to the kingship. But we have seen his respect for "the LORD's anointed" in both the encounters with Saul, and this allows us to think that he is being portrayed as "the man after God's own heart." Both Joseph and David, therefore, display a sense that God has good purposes that it is incumbent on them to promote, even at cost to themselves.

22. I have explored this in McConville, "Forgiveness."
23. So, for example, Sarna, *Genesis*, 293-94; also Jacobs, "Conceptual Dynamics," 326.

Conclusion

The Old Testament locates the concept of forgiveness in God's ordering of the world for flourishing and justice. Sin militates against this, creating deficiencies that must be put right. Instances of human forgiveness are intelligible in this theological context.

A key measure of human forgiveness, therefore, is the subject's intention regarding outcomes. Does it matter whether the subject *feels* forgiving? The narratives we have considered suggest not. Human forgiveness seeks to put things right at a higher level than the person's own narrow interests. Yet we have noticed in the case of Joseph an interplay between the private and the public man, a strong emotive element that breaks through the carefully constructed, inscrutable exterior at key moments. In the David narrative, comprising the Saul and Nabal episodes, we noted an aspect of character formation. Here too, apparently, the disposition of the agent matters. In both cases, the narrative implies an inner struggle to do the right thing and a readiness to accept personal cost.[24]

The point lies close to the idea of forgiveness as therapeutic. This, indeed, is implied in the Sirach text we noticed earlier: "Does anyone harbor [*suntērei*] anger against another, and expect healing from the LORD?" (Sir 28:3). The passage develops its basic postulate of a reciprocity between receiving forgiveness from God and offering it to others (vv. 2–4) and exhorts the faithful to place personal animosities in the perspective of the whole of life and of God's commandments (vv. 6–7). Then, tellingly, it goes on to expose the damaging effects of nourishing rancor:

> Refrain from strife and your sins will be fewer;
> For the hot-tempered kindle strife. (Sir 28:8, NRSV)

The passage therefore recognizes a therapeutic dimension of forgiveness, which can arguably also be found in the Joseph and David narratives. But it may be that the decision to embark on a path of reconciliation and

---

24. In a documentary aired on the BBC, *My Dad, the Peace Deal, and Me*, Patrick Kielty, the comedian and host of *Love Island*, expressed this tension between the public and the private sharply and poignantly. He forgives the sectarian murderers of his father (in the Northern Ireland troubles) in order to enable a return to peaceable relations in the community. He clarifies that he does not forgive on his own behalf and cannot do that; rather, he simply absorbs the hurt ("sucks it up"), so that he can catch the wave of the new opportunities enabled by the Good Friday Agreement. In this way, he chooses to be part of the mending of things, the building of a new, better way of living together (Burley, *My Dad*).

mutual reconstruction precedes, perhaps becomes an instrument of, the emotional therapy.

There is in addition a question about the nature of justice and, therefore, the justification of forgiveness. The issue is not clear cut. Terrible deeds *matter*, and it would be a perverse reading of the Old Testament to think otherwise. It is a profound wrong to "heal the wound of my people lightly" (Jer 8:11). Yet healing is another metaphor within the sphere of forgiveness and restoration, and the divine purpose to heal, in the Old Testament narrative, always finally trumps the divine purpose to punish (cf. Hos 11:8–9). Even God's anger is motivated by his vision of the well-being of people in his world. In this, human beings are surely called to be his imitators. Divine forgiveness aims to enable continuing life and flourishing, and it follows that human forgiveness has the same goal. If my former enemies want to work with me for the common good, then I must work with them. I must rise above my own rancor and also assume their goodwill, as long as it is plausible to do so.

9

Forgiveness in the Christian Scriptures

Sinai, Golgotha, and Beyond

ANTHONY BASH

Interpersonal Forgiveness in the Hebrew Bible

HANNAH ARENDT, THE POLITICAL philosopher, observed in 1958 that the "discoverer of the role of forgiveness in the realm of human affairs was Jesus of Nazareth."[1] Arendt was a secular Jew and probably wrote from within her experience of the Judeo-Christian tradition. In support of Arendt's views, we can suggest three simple observations about the Hebrew Bible. First, concepts that are important in the Christian Scriptures for explaining forgiveness—concepts that are expressed, for example, by words such as moral, virtues, and emotions—appear to be absent in the Hebrew Bible. Second, in the Hebrew Bible, there are not commands or exhortations urging people to forgive one another. Last, there are not examples of discrete words or phrases that seem to refer to people forgiving one another. Taken together, these observations have led people like Arendt to conclude that interpersonal forgiveness was not a form of behavior known to or practiced by the ancient Jews.

---

1. Arendt, *Human Condition*, 238.

As for the absence of words such as morals, virtues, or emotions in relation to forgiveness, it is anachronistic to expect to find them in the periods during which the Hebrew Scriptures came together, for two reasons. First, because the idea of morals and virtues and the ways the writers of the Christian Scriptures thought about them have grown out of the traditions of Greek ethics. Second, *emotions* is a relatively modern term for referring to the full range of feelings that human beings experience.

We can certainly say that in the Hebrew Bible, there is thought and reflection about how to live and act well in an ethical sense, but the thinking is from within religious, cultural, historical, and social traditions that are different from both ancient Greek traditions and in the Christian Scriptures.[2] As for emotions, there is evidence that ancient Jews felt and had labels for some of the affective responses that are today called emotions.[3] The absence of terms now used to describe and refer to the characteristics and attributes of forgiveness does not mean the ancient Israelites did not forgive.

When we consider the second observation (that there are not commands or exhortations to forgive others in the Hebrew Bible), it is true that interpersonal forgiveness is not explicitly celebrated or commanded as a way of godly behavior in the way that it is in the Christian Scriptures. It is also true that (as we shall see) there are few, if any, examples of interpersonal forgiveness in the Hebrew Scriptures that fit with the way interpersonal forgiveness is thought about in the Christian Scriptures. But this does not mean people were not forgiving in ancient Israel or that they did not regard forgiving others as sometimes right and a way of being righteous and of doing God's will. What we cannot assume is that when, why, and how the ancient Israelites thought it is right to forgive will correspond with later views about when it is right to forgive—and neither can we necessarily criticize the ancient Israelites for forgiving differently from people in a later period.

As for the last observation (that there is no language for interpersonal forgiveness in the Hebrew Bible), it is a mistake to suppose that the ancient Israelites did not forgive one another, simply because we cannot identify a word or concept that corresponds with language explicitly denoting

2. For an important study on the ethics of the ancient Israelites, see Barton, *Ethics in Ancient Israel*. A reviewer of Barton's book commented that the "Israelites . . . were thinking about ethics, were in the habit of moral reasoning, before Socrates was born" (Van De Wiele, "Book Review," 105.)

3. On the nature of what in Hebrew thought are now called emotions, see Mirguet, "What Is an 'Emotion'?" 442 and 464–65 esp., and Spencer, *Mixed Feelings*. I discuss this question further in ch. 2 of Bash, *Remorse*.

interpersonal forgiveness. The absence of a word or phrase to describe interpersonal forgiveness does not mean that people did not forgive one another. To use a modern example, people may not know what *trichotillomania* or *iktsuarpok* are, but this does not mean that trichotillomania or iktsuarpok do not exist as feelings and behaviors.[4]

Despite the apparent paucity of records and examples, we shall see that it is very likely that the ancient Jews did forgive one another on occasions.[5] To adapt Arendt's wording, the ancient Jews *had* discovered the role of forgiveness in their affairs, though from within their own culture and traditions. We illustrate the point with some observations from the lives of Joseph and David.

Joseph

Joseph and his brothers in Gen 50:15–21 are an obvious example of what some regard as interpersonal forgiveness. But in which senses are they an example, if at all? Joseph's brothers falsely told Joseph that Jacob's dying wish had been for Joseph to forgive his brothers for the wrongs they had done to him. The word translated "forgive" in v. 17 is נשׂא (lift up, bear, take away, carry), which in some places is used figuratively to describe God's forgiveness of sins.[6] Joseph's response to Jacob's supposed request is that he is not in the place of God. In other words, he saw forgiving as a divine act. The implication, as we shall also see below, is that human beings may overlook or pardon others' wrongs, but forgiving in the way God does is, not surprisingly, for God alone. Despite saying it was not his role to forgive his brothers' wrongs, Joseph did not exact revenge on his brothers but comforted, spoke kindly to, and agreed to provide for his brothers (v. 21).

4. Respectively, they are (i) a compulsive desire or behavior to pull out one's hair, and (ii) the feeling of anticipation of waiting for someone to arrive, often coupled with the urge to check to see if the person has arrived.

5. This is in keeping with an unverified (and unverifiable) general observation widely made that forgiveness, whether looked at diachronically or synchronically, seems to be a universal human phenomenon.

6. In two places, priests in their role as God's representatives are asked to remove sin against God as part of the role to make atonement (Exod 28:38 and Lev 10:17.) The verb used is נשׂא. The verb commonly used of God's forgiveness is סלח. Besides נשׂא, other words or phrases are used to express something of the same idea: see, e.g., כפר (piel: cover), כבס (piel: cleanse), מחה (blot out), רפא (heal, restore), שלך (hiphil: cast behind one's back), סתר (hiphil: conceal from), עבר (hiphil: take away, let pass by), תהר (piel: purify), and לא זכר (not to remember).

In other words, much the same outcome as we might have expected to see of forgiveness in the contemporary period is in evidence, in the context of Joseph's denial that it was not possible for him to offer forgiveness, since offering forgiveness is in the gift of God, not human beings.

David

David is not explicitly described as being forgiving, but sometimes his behavior has similarities with what we might call forgiveness. We look at five examples, three of which concern Absalom, one of David's sons.

Absalom had a sister, Tamar, and a half-brother, Ammon, all children of David. Ammon raped Tamar, his half-sister. Two years later, Absalom instigated the murder of Ammon in revenge for the rape. Absalom was forced to flee into exile for the murder. He was restored to Jerusalem after three years of exile. A further two-year period elapsed before David was persuaded to meet Absalom again (2 Sam 13:34—14:33,) even though David had mourned for Absalom when he was in exile and had longed for his return (2 Sam 13:37–39.) David kissed Absalom on Absalom's return to the court, and the text implies—but does not state explicitly—forgiveness and reconciliation.

The interpretation of this story is made less straightforward because of 2 Sam 13:39, which indicates that David was "comforted" by the news of Absalom's revenge on his (Absalom's) half-brother, Ammon. David's subsequent forgiveness of Absalom (if David's response is properly to be called forgiveness) is probably Absalom's restoration to David with David having waived his (David's) right to retribution against Absalom for Absalom's murder of Ammon. It is probably also David's implicit acknowledgement that Absalom had a right to revenge. Such an interpretation of ancient Israelite forgiveness—that forgiveness is in part to waive the right to revenge—reinforces the interpretation I offer below about forgiveness in the period of Jesus.

Another example is the way David treats Shimei, the son of Gera and a member of Saul's family. Shimei cursed David and threw stones at David as David was fleeing Jerusalem (2 Sam 16:5–14) during Absalom's rebellion (2 Sam 15:1—19:43.) After Absalom's defeat and death, Shimei met David, acknowledged that he had done wrong, and asked for mercy. David chose not to take revenge and (from a modern viewpoint) appears to pardon Shimei. There is nothing in the text that explicitly suggests that David forgave the wrong done to him (2 Sam 19:16–23), even though the outcomes of David's actions are much the same as if, in later practice, he had forgiven Shimei. Once again, we see that forgiveness amounts to waiving the right to revenge.

Third, Mephibosheth, the grandson of Saul, had a servant named Ziba. During Absalom's rebellion, according to Ziba, Mephibosheth did not support David, in the hope that he (Mephibosheth) would be restored to Saul's kingdom (2 Sam 16:1–4.) After the rebellion, Mephibosheth claimed Ziba had misled him and misrepresented him to David. David did not avenge himself on either Ziba or Mephibosheth. Clearly, David did not know which of the two to believe and so took revenge on neither. Certainly, David overlooked the wrongs, and this could suggest a form of forgiveness (2 Sam 19:24–30.)

Last, we have two examples that illustrate ancient forgiveness as a form of reciprocal exchange. In 1 Sam 25:23–35, Abigail pleads with David for mercy on account of the behavior of Nabal, her husband, towards David. In exchange for gifts (v. 35), David accepts her entreaty for mercy and spares Nabal and his household (vv. 33–34). But we should note that it was not Abigail who had done wrong but Nabal, and the "forgiveness," such as it may be, is offered as part of a process of reciprocal exchange.

The same idea of reciprocal exchange is evident in Exod 10:17–18. In response to Pharaoh's acknowledgment to Moses that he had "sinned against your God and against you," Pharaoh asked Moses to "forgive" his sin (the verb used is נשא) and to mediate with God for God to drive away the locusts that were destroying Egypt's plants and vegetation. In other words, Pharaoh sought a stipulated benefit, a quid pro quo, for admitting he had done wrong.[7]

Reasons for the Paucity of Examples

If the Israelites were to be holy as God is holy, why were they not also to be forgiving, as God is forgiving? If they were to love their neighbors, why were they not also to forgive them, and why did people not think that it

---

7. According to the contemporary approach to forgiveness, forgiveness can be sought only for one's own wrongdoing and is typically regarded as a gift, given without price. The unconditioned nature of forgiveness is particularly emphasized by Derrida in *On Cosmopolitanism and Forgiveness*.

was loving to forgive and overlook wrongs that that they suffered from their neighbors?[8]

One reason might be that the ancient Israelites did not regard interpersonal forgiveness so important or noteworthy as to highlight it in oral traditions or writing. Another might be that the forgiving behavior of the ancient Israelites has some significant differences from forgiving behavior as described in the Christian Scriptures. It is not that the ancient Israelites did not forgive; it is that they forgave differently. We might say that their behavior bears a "family resemblance" to what is meant by forgiveness in the Christian Scriptures but is not identical to it.[9]

More specifically and as I have already said of Joseph, interpersonal forgiveness is treated in the Hebrew Scriptures differently from the way it is treated in the Christian Scriptures after the time of Jesus. This is because forgiveness was then understood to be something God does and that human beings cannot and should not dare to arrogate to themselves the right or the power to forgive others. Even the Gospels show evidence of this sort of approach.[10] Perhaps we see the same thing in the Lord's Prayer in Luke's Gospel where God forgives sins, but people forgive debts.[11]

It is not surprising that language about forgiveness is linked to language about debt (in the sense of reciprocal obligations and rights), for at least three reasons. First, because Christian forgiveness grew out of a culture that sometimes quantified the compensation that wrongdoers owed their victims as a result of crimes and other misdemeanors. Second, because in that culture, also specified was what had to be offered to God in sacrifice for wrongs. Last, ancient Israelite culture permitted (proportionate) revenge, with a victim entitled to exact the equivalent of a debt from the wrongdoer. Well known is the context of Jewish and other ancient Near Eastern laws in the period of the Hebrew Scriptures that typically set out a measured right to

8. This approach was suggested in Barton, "Understanding Old Testament Ethics," and E. Davies, "Walking in God's Ways," but has been latterly discounted among scholars.

9. The term "family resemblance" was made popular by Wittgenstein in *Philosophical Investigations*. Applied to forgiveness, it means that forgiveness may not have one essential common feature but may be a variety of forms of behavior that are connected by a series of overlapping similarities, but with no one feature common to every type of forgiveness.

10. See Mark 2:1–12.

11. This perhaps may reflect a play on the Hebrew verb נשׁה, which means *both* to lend (or to become a creditor) *and* to forget. In Matthew, people forgive debts, and so does God, so my suggestion is not watertight. But this point holds good: there was nervousness about saying that people forgave sins.

retribution or retaliation in response to wrongdoing. The retaliation can be "an eye for an eye, a tooth for a tooth,"[12] but no more. In such a context, the social, cultic, and legal framework of ancient Jewish life militated against the development of an explicitly formulated ethic of interpersonal forgiveness.

The Intertestamental Period

Despite what is popularly thought, there was not a "leap" from the Hebrew Scriptures to the Christian Scriptures when it comes to interpersonal forgiveness. There are some important sociocultural developments in the period between the close of the Hebrew Scriptures and the start of the Christian Scriptures that indicate a reshaping of the way the Jews thought of interpersonal forgiveness. By the time of Jesus, an apparently well-articulated approach to the importance of interpersonal forgiveness was already part of the Jewish wisdom tradition, though how widespread and how well known is difficult to say. For example, we know of interpersonal forgiveness in Ecclesiasticus, an early second-century BCE text. Sirach 28:1–5 clearly refers to interpersonal forgiveness. In v. 2, for example, ben Sira says, "Forgive the wrongdoing your neighbor has done to you." There is also evidence of an established practice of interpersonal forgiveness among the Jews in the time of Jesus. In Matt 18:21, for example, Peter quotes an existing (and presumably well-established) tradition that the subjects of wrongdoing should forgive those who wronged them up to seven times.[13]

The Jewish Base of the Christian Scriptures

The Christian Scriptures follow some of the patterns of thought about forgiveness that we see in the Hebrew Scriptures. For example, forgiveness is not always the explicitly stated route to restored relationships. Just as David was reconciled to Absalom, Shimei, and Mephibosheth without explicit mention of forgiveness, so Jesus urges those who remember that someone has something against them to go to be "reconciled," without any mention of antecedent forgiveness (Matt 5:24).

12. As in Exod 21:23–25 and Lev 24:19–21. The same is true of the Babylonian Code of Hammurabi (c. 1754 BCE).

13. If the early Christians thought that Jesus introduced interpersonal forgiveness *de novo* as a pattern of behavior, Matthew would not have indicated that it was already well established in Jewish thought.

In the Hebrew Scriptures, repentance precedes divine forgiveness. Repentance for sin remains at the heart of Christian spirituality, just as it is in Jewish spirituality in the Hebrew Scriptures. In keeping with this, John's baptism was a baptism of *repentance* for the forgiveness of sins (Mark 1:4).[14] This pattern of antecedent repentance as the prerequisite of divine forgiveness is the usual pattern of interpersonal forgiveness.

Of course, there are radical departures from the Hebrew Scriptures too. For example, in Matt 9:2–8,[15] the scribes are critical that Jesus told a paralyzed man that his sins were forgiven. The scribes regard this statement as "blasphemy," because Jesus appears to overlook the place of sacrifices for sins committed unintentionally, the ritual of the Day of Atonement, and the place of prayer to God for mercy for sins deliberately committed. Jesus adds that "the son of man has authority on earth to forgive sins" (v. 6.) We are not told what the reaction of scribes was, but almost certainly they continued to "think evil" in their hearts (v. 4).

Additionally, from a pattern of relationships that is based on interpersonal reciprocity—an eye for an eye and a tooth for a tooth (Matt 5:38)—Jesus sets out a pattern of relationships that is based on the reciprocity of the experience of grace, for as God has forgiven people their sins, so the recipients of God's forgiveness are now to forgive others their sins (Matt 18:23–35).[16] Were it otherwise, the experience of divine forgiveness would not be contingent on faith and grace.

An important development—but not a departure—from the Hebrew Scriptures is the way Jesus restates the law and its purpose. While insisting that he had not come to abolish "the law and the prophets" (Matt 5:17), Jesus took two passages form the Hebrew Scriptures as his starting point for a hermeneutical framework. The first is Lev 19:17–18, where hate, vengeance, and grudges are proscribed and love for one's neighbor required. The second is Lev 19:34, which required people to treat others in the way they themselves would like to be treated and to love such people—even refugees—as themselves (Lev 19:34). These axioms became the framework of an ethic that is based on a reinterpretation and (sometimes) intensification of the law in the Hebrew Scriptures. It is easy to see how an ethic

14. Hence Mark 4:12b. See also Luke 3:3, 17:3–4.

15. See // Mark 2:1–11 and Luke 5:17–26.

16. Matthew 6:12, 14–15, interpreted on the basis of Matt 18:23–25. On the woman who was a "sinner" who was touched by God's forgiveness, see Luke 7:36–49. See also Mark 11:25–26; Luke 6:37.

of interpersonal forgiveness came out of this new approach, for to forgive another means that one sets aside one's hatred, desire for vengeance, and grudges—and replaces these feelings not with surly acceptance of the other but with grace-filled love.

Forgiveness in the Christian Scriptures

How, then, is interpersonal forgiveness explained and described in the Christian Scriptures?[17] There is no obvious model in the Hebrew Scriptures on which to draw. Paul, the earliest Christian writer, uses the verb *charizomai* to describe interpersonal forgiveness and by it understands forgiveness to be a loving gift of grace either in a person-to-person context or in a community setting. It is a term describing the response of people towards repentant people—we see this in 2 Cor 2:7, 10—and in the later letters ascribed to Paul, it is used to describe the way to deal with awkward people in the church community. Just as people have received grace through the Christ-event, so they are to practice grace in their relationships with one another.[18] The idea of reciprocal exchange motivated by grace is one explanation of the way forgiveness is described.

It is a matter of debate how much Paul knew of Jesus's teaching. The idea of interpersonal forgiveness is integral to Jesus's teaching, and I doubt that Paul was unaware of it. However, the way Paul writes about interpersonal forgiveness is different from the way Jesus talks of it. For Jesus, in the translated (from Aramaic to Greek) language of the Gospels, forgiveness is described by a verb, *aphiēmi*, and the cognate noun, *aphesis*. These words existed in secular Greek, and they mean "to leave, to let go" and were already in use in the LXX of divine forgiveness. Interpersonal forgiveness in this sense is to let go of one's right to revenge and retribution that the *lex talionis* permitted.[19]

---

17. I have explored these questions at length in Bash, *Forgiveness and Christian Ethics; Just Forgiveness;* and *Forgiveness.*

18. E.g., Eph 4:32; Col 3:13. *Charizomai* can also refer to the cancellation of a debt (e.g., Luke 7:42–43) or the bestowal of a favour or other kind of undeserved kindness (e.g., Luke 7:21.)

19. There is another verb for forgiveness that Luke once uses, *apoluō*, and it means much the same as *aphiēmi*, with the emphasis on releasing someone from someone or something. An interesting passage is Acts 3, where in the space of seven verses, *apoluō* is used in v. 13 (in the sense of "release") and *charizomai* is used in v. 14 (in the sense of "be granted"). The word does not mean "to forgive" in either case.

There are some who read an ethic of unconditional forgiveness in the Christian Scriptures. By this, I mean an ethic that treats as virtuous those who forgive the unrepentant. Often taken as paradigmatic of this approach are Jesus's words on the cross in Luke 23:34. I think this is a mistake. The words are not an example of Jesus forgiving the unrepentant but (in keeping with the pattern of thought in the Hebrew Scriptures)[20] an example of Jesus praying that God would forgive those who had sinned not intentionally but in ignorance.[21] In all likelihood, people are not to forgive their unrepentant neighbors (we discuss why below), though of course they should love them and pray for them (Matt 5:44), as Jesus says in the context of his abrogation of the ethic of the *lex talionis* in Matt 5:38. Within the Christian Scriptures, repentance and forgiveness usually go together and stand in a reciprocal relationship.

There is, of course, a categorical difference between divine forgiveness and interpersonal forgiveness, most obviously because at the eschaton, God will reverse and put right the effects of sin; whereas with interpersonal forgiveness, we face what Arendt has called "the predicament of irreversibility."[22] In using the same word, forgiveness, for both, we are referring to something that is related but not the same. This is where I think Anne C. Minas went wrong in an article in which she argued that cannot God cannot forgive sins.[23] She took as her starting point the definition of forgiveness in the *Oxford English Dictionary*, which more or less describes interpersonal forgiveness as understood today, and (in effect) showed that God's forgiveness cannot be the same as interpersonal forgiveness. To this extent, she is right. But she went on to say that since God cannot forgive in this way, God cannot forgive at all. On this, she is wrong. Based on her premise—that God's forgiveness is the same as interpersonal forgiveness—her reasoning is flawless. However, her premise is wrong: God's forgiveness is not the same as interpersonal forgiveness, and it is a mistake to regard the two as the same.

20. E.g., Lev 4:1–25, Num 15:22–31, reflected in Heb 6:4, 10:26.

21. See Acts 3:17.

22. Arendt, *Human Condition*, 246. In context, Arendt suggests that the "faculty of forgiving" is the "possible redemption from the predicament of irreversibility," but in this I believe she is mistaken, as interpersonal forgiveness cannot undo the fact of the wrongdoing. Victim and wrongdoer are irreversibly changed by the fact of the wrongdoing, for it is only ever a wronged victim who forgives and (typically) a repentant wrongdoer who is forgiven.

23. Minas, "God and Forgiveness." I discuss the article in Bash, "Forgiveness."

Charizomai, aphiēmi, and *aphesis* are used of divine forgiveness in the Christian Scriptures, just as they are of interpersonal forgiveness. In addition, at least three other words are used to describe divine forgiveness. The words are, first, *athetesis* (Heb 9:26), referring to the "removal" or "setting aside" of sin through the sacrificial death of Jesus,[24] and, second, *paresis* (Rom 3:25), referring to God "passing over" sins. (In extra-biblical literature, *paresis* is used in much the way *aphesis* is used and often refers to the remission of debts.) Lastly, the verb *exaleiphō* is used twice, once in Acts 3:19 (where forgiveness is described as "wiping away sins"—*exaleiphō hamartias*) and once in Col 2:14 (*exaleiphō to cheirographon*—wiping away or cancelling the written record of one's debts [against God]) and taking away (*airō*) the written record, nailing it to the cross. In this latter verse, forgiveness is seen as being like the erasure of the legal record of debts.

Paul thinks of salvation in terms of reconciliation and justification, not forgiveness. He explicitly refers to divine forgiveness by a word that can be translated "forgiveness" in only one verse (Rom 4:7, in a quotation from Ps 32:1), though, of course, Paul's explanations of justification—namely, that God thereby covers and does not reckon sin (Rom 4:7–8)—amount to a gloss on what it means to forgive.

Each of the Gospels looks on divine forgiveness in different ways. In Mark's Gospel, the gospel is good news about a person, Jesus Christ, who brings about the kingdom of God, begun in the present and awaiting its full expression in the future; the good news is not principally about forgiveness. It is in and through this person that God mediates ransom (Mark 10:45), presumably for redemption. In the new order of the kingdom, sins will be forgiven (Mark 4:12). In the present, there is a foretaste of these future realities. So, when in Mark 2:5 Jesus says to the paralytic that his sins are forgiven, he is pointing to a future reality of which the paralytic could be certain and which he could, to some extent, experience in the present. So, forgiveness of sins is a future certainty, linked to a person, to the kingdom he establishes, and to the gift of his life as a ransom. In addition, and as both John the Baptist and Jesus say, entering or receiving the kingdom depends on antecedent repentance.[25] By implication, the temple order with its sacrifices and priesthood is irrelevant in the new order of the kingdom.

24. The same word occurs in Heb 7:18, where the word's meaning as a legal technical term is borrowed and refers to the "abrogation" or "annulment" of an earlier statement by a subsequent statement.

25. Mark 1:4, 15. See also Mark 4:11–12, which explicitly links the kingdom, repentance, and forgiveness.

As forgiveness is one of the characteristics of the kingdom, it is inconceivable that its members should not also model the ethic of the kingdom and themselves be forgivers. This explains why Jesus says in Mark 11:25 that his followers are to forgive if they have "anything against anyone." The result will be that God will forgive forgivers their trespasses. This is not to say that divine forgiveness is contingent on the practice of interpersonal forgiveness; rather, it is that those who live in the grace of the kingdom will practice and mediate the grace of the kingdom towards others and will themselves be recipients of God's forgiveness. If they are not forgivers, they thereby demonstrate that they have not received the kingdom and so will not receive the forgiveness of God.[26]

In Luke's Gospel, the kingdom is not the central organizing principle. Rather, it is that Jesus is "the Christ" (Messiah) who is Savior (Luke 2:11) and who brings both salvation and *aphesis* (Luke 1:77). Luke does not intend only forgiveness when he uses the world *aphesis*. We see this clearly in Luke 4:18 (quoting Isa 61:1–2) where on the two occasions when *aphesis* is used, it is translated by words such as liberty, restoration, or freedom. By *aphesis*, Luke is describing the way that God releases people from the effects of sin—illness and death, demonic forces, oppression, and injustice—both in their experience of the present and future worlds. The key idea is that with Jesus comes *aphesis*—release, restoration, freedom, forgiveness.[27] *Aphesis* is therefore shorthand for the way God reorders the present human experience that has been corrupted by sin, a process that begins in the present and that will be completed at the eschaton. Human beings also take part in and model that ministry, addressing injustice, oppression, cruelty, and wrongdoing—a ministry that I think should be called "aphetic," reflecting that God's people share in striving for *aphesis* in the present in response to the gospel and as God's co-workers.[28]

Matthew's Gospel also makes a distinctive contribution to a theology of forgiveness. In Matt 26:28, Matthew adds the words "for the forgiveness of sins" to the words of institution in the Lord's Supper when Jesus takes the cup. The wine is a symbol of "the blood of the covenant, which is poured out for many, for the forgiveness of sins." Forgiveness is here rooted not so

26. This is the framework for interpreting Matt 6:12 and Luke 11:4.

27. Luke is also drawing on the theology such as we see in Isa 58:6–12, for example.

28. Some (mistakenly, in my view) say that Luke does not have a theology of the atonement. I think they are wrong, and spectacularly so! It is in, through, and by faith in Christ, the Messiah, that atonement comes, and that necessarily means faith in him, in his life, death, and resurrection.

much in a person (as in Mark), or in the kingdom (as in Luke), but in the death of Jesus ("blood"), which is like the sacrifices of the Hebrew Scriptures ("poured out") that sealed a "covenant" and brings about "forgiveness of sins." Matthew makes an explicit link between Jesus's death and the forgiveness of sins, which Mark and Luke do not do.

At this point, we should remember that the regular patterns of temple sacrifices in the Hebrew Scriptures were ways that the relationship between God's people and God were renewed.[29] What Matthew is alluding to in the words of institution is a once-for-all sacrifice that sealed a covenant for forgiveness, in much the same way that the sacrifices in Exod 24 sealed the covenant at Sinai. We should note, too, that Matthew also omits any idea that repentance as a result of responding to the preaching of John the Baptist could lead to the forgiveness of sins, because he omits the words "for the forgiveness of sins" from John's message. Matthew wants to make it clear that by his death Jesus sealed a new covenant and that forgiveness of sins lay at the center of the new covenant.

John's Gospel is more or less silent on divine forgiveness. The only explicit allusion to divine forgiveness is in John 20:23. John seems to presuppose an institutional setting for granting and being granted forgiveness, with God forgiving those whom the apostles forgive and God "retaining"— I assume this means "not forgiving"—the sins that the apostles retain. This approach to forgiveness and to the atonement seems at variance with much else that we see about divine forgiveness in the Christian Scriptures, but there is a strand of thinking in the Christian Scriptures that points to the apostles in some senses being brokers of forgiveness; see 1 Cor 4:3–5, Matt 16:19, and 18:18, for example.

In 1 John, God forgives those who confess their sins (1 John 1:9) and divine forgiveness comes "on account of [Jesus's] name" (1 John 2:12.) The language about Jesus's death in 1 John 1:7, 2:2, and 4:10 strongly suggests that the writer understands Jesus's death to be an atoning sacrifice for sins that brings about forgiveness. In this respect, the theology of the atonement in 1 John is much like the theology of Matthew in his Gospel, though with the emphasis on sacrifice rather than on covenant.

---

29. In contrast, in Heb 9:22, the writer does seem to understand the Jewish sacrifices as being for the forgiveness of sins.

Summary and Conclusions

Interpersonal forgiveness in the Christian Scriptures is set in the theology and ethics of the Hebrew Scriptures and is a development of them. The Christian Scriptures explore new ways to understand what forgiveness is, why people should forgive one another, what happens if people do not forgive one another, and how God forgives human sins. Examples of interpersonal forgiveness are implicit in the Hebrew Scriptures. Explicit, written evidence of interpersonal forgiveness in Jewish practice and traditions exists from as early as the start of the second century BCE.

In some parts of the Christian Scriptures, especially the Synoptic Gospels, interpersonal forgiveness comes out of a new interpretation of the ethics of the Hebrew Scriptures. In effect, Jesus abrogated the *lex talionis* and reinterpreted the command to love one's neighbor (Lev 19:18) as also including an obligation to forgive one's neighbor. Within the setting of the Gospels and of contemporary Jewish thought, the starting point of forgiveness is primarily *not* to do something (to take revenge or to insist on what one is entitled to) rather than, as in a modern setting, *to do* something, such as to forswear resentment.[30] To some extent, forgiveness remains in a reciprocal setting but in a limited way, with God's forgiveness transforming forgiven people into becoming forgivers themselves who thereby become all the more sure of God's forgiveness at the eschaton. It is also reciprocal in the sense of typically being a response to antecedent repentance.

The kingdom of God in Mark and Luke is in inchoate form in the present and will be fully realized in the future. God's reordering of the effects of sin are anticipated and to some extent experienced in the present. Believers are to model God's future forgiveness by themselves practicing forgiveness in the present.

Paul derives an ethic of interpersonal forgiveness from the grace of the Christ-event: just as God has called and sustains believers through grace, so believers, as recipients of God's grace, are to mediate that grace to others. To "gift with grace" someone, which is how we might paraphrase *charizomai*, means we do things that we also call forgiving.

As for how God forgives human sins, Matthew roots God's forgiveness in Jesus's death and sees the death as sealing a new covenant for forgiveness. Paul reconfigures how to understand the atonement with the language of

---

30. The latter phrase is found in sermons 8 and 9 (136–67) of Bishop Butler's *Fifteen Sermons* and has been taken to be the starting point of the modern study of forgiveness.

justification and so barely alludes to God's forgiveness. In the first letter of John, the writer affirms that Jesus's death is an atoning sacrifice.

Finally, Jesus is not the "discoverer of the role of forgiveness in the realm of human affairs" (*pace* Arendt). Nevertheless, when it comes to forgiveness, Jesus's achievement is twofold. First, he articulated a new framework for understanding and exploring a type of interpersonal behavior that is (just about) evident in the Hebrew Scriptures. Second, he set this type of behavior in a reinterpreted hermeneutic of the Hebrew Scriptures. One result is that forgiveness (whether in its first-century or later forms) is now regarded as an important constituent of reconciliation and of the restoration of disrupted relationships.

Bibliography

Achenbach, Reinhard. "Complementary Reading of the Torah in the Priestly Texts of Numbers 15." In *Torah and the Book of Numbers*, edited by Christian Frevel et al., 201–32. FAT 2/62. Tübingen: Mohr Siebeck, 2013.

Alter, Robert. *The David Story: A Translation with Commentary of 1 and 2 Samuel.* New York: Norton & Co, 1999.

Anderson, Gary A. *Charity: The Place of the Poor in the Biblical Tradition.* New Haven, CT: Yale University Press, 2013.

———. *Christian Doctrine and the Old Testament: Theology in the Service of Biblical Exegesis.* Grand Rapids: Baker Academic, 2017.

———. "The Interpretation of the Purification Offering (חטאת) in the Temple Scroll (11QTemple) and Rabbinic Literature." *JBL* 111 (1992) 17–35.

———. *Sin: A History.* New Haven, CT: Yale University Press, 2009.

Annus, Amar, and Alan Lenzi. *Ludlul bēl nēmeqi: The Standard Babylonian Poem of the Righteous Sufferer.* SAACT 7. Helsinki: University of Helsinki Press, 2010.

Anscombe, Gertrude Elizabeth Margaret. *Intention.* Cambridge: Harvard University Press, 1957.

Arendt, Hannah. *The Human Condition.* 2nd ed. Chicago: University of Chicago Press, 1998.

Arnold, Bill T., and John H. Choi. *A Guide to Biblical Hebrew Syntax.* Cambridge: Cambridge University Press, 2003.

Artus, Olivier. *Études sur le livre des Nombres: Récit, Histoire et Loi en Nb 13,1—20,13.* OBO 157. Göttingen: Editions Universitaire, 1997.

Ashley, Timothy R. *The Book of Numbers.* NICOT. Grand Rapids: Eerdmans, 1993.

Auld, Graeme. *I & II Samuel.* OTL. Louisville, KY: Westminster John Knox, 2011.

Baden, Joel S. "The Structure and Substance of Numbers 15." *VT* 63 (2013) 351–67.

Baldwin, Joyce. *1 and 2 Samuel: An Introduction and Commentary.* TOTC. Leicester, UK: InterVarsity, 1988.

Balentine, S. E. "My Servant Job Shall Pray for You." *Theology Today* 58 (2002) 502–18.

Barth, C. "ליץ." In *TDOT*, 7:547–52.

Barton, John. *Ethics in Ancient Israel*. Oxford: Oxford University Press, 2014.

———. "Understanding Old Testament Ethics." *JSOT* 9 (1978) 44–64.

Bash, Anthony. *Forgiveness and Christian Ethics*. Cambridge: Cambridge University Press, 2007.

———. "Forgiveness: A Re-Appraisal." *Studies in Christian Ethics* 24 (2011) 1–14.

———. *Forgiveness: A Theology*. Cascade Companions. Eugene, OR: Cascade, 2015.

———. *Just Forgiveness: Exploring the Bible, Weighing the Issues*. London: SPCK, 2011.

———. *Remorse: A Christian Perspective*. Eugene, OR: Cascade, 2020.

Batto, Bernard F. "The Reed Sea: *Requiescat in Pace*." In *In the Beginning: Essays on Creation Myths in the Ancient Near East and the Bible*, 158–74. Siphrut: Literature and Theology of the Hebrew Scriptures 9. Winona Lake, IN: Eisenbrauns, 2013.

Bellis, Alice Ogden, and Joel S. Kaminsky, eds. *Jews, Christians, and the Theology of the Hebrew Scriptures*. Society of Biblical Literature Symposium 8. Atlanta: Society of Biblical Literature, 2000.

Biddle, Mark. "Ancestral Motifs in 1 Samuel 25: Intertextuality and Characterization." *JBL* 121 (2002) 617–38.

Block, Daniel I. *Judges, Ruth*. NAC 6. Nashville: B&H, 1999.

Boda, Mark J. *A Severe Mercy: Sin and its Remedy in the Old Testament*. Siphrut: Literature and Theology of the Hebrew Scriptures 1. Winona Lake, IN: Eisenbrauns, 2009.

Brenner, A. "Job the Pious? The Characterization of Job in the Narrative Framework of the Book." *JSOT* 43 (1989) 37–52.

Brichto, Herbert Chanan. *Toward a Grammar of Biblical Poetics: Tales of the Prophets*. New York: Oxford University Press, 1992.

Bridge, Edward J. "Desperation to a Desperado: Abigail's Request to David in 1 Samuel 25." *ABR* 63 (2015) 14–28.

Brueggemann, Walter. *1 & 2 Kings*. Macon, GA: Smyth & Helwys, 2000.

Budde, Karl. *Das Buch Hiob*. HKAT II.1. Göttingen: Vandenhoeck & Ruprecht, 1896.

Burley, Leo, dir. *My Dad, the Peace Deal, and Me*. London: Dragonfly, 2018.

Butler, Joseph. *Fifteen Sermons Preached at the Rolls' Chapel*, edited by William E. Gladstone. Vol. 2 of *The Works of Joseph Butler*. Reprint, Bristol: Thoemmes, 1995.

Campbell, Antony J. *1 Samuel*. FOTL 7. Grand Rapids: Eerdmans, 2003.

Caquot, André, and Philippe de Robert. *Les livres de Samuel*. Geneva: Labor et Fides, 1994.

Chapman, Stephen B. *1 Samuel as Christian Scripture: A Theological Commentary*. Grand Rapids: Eerdmans, 2016.

Clines, D. J. A. "Coming to a Theological Conclusion: The Case of the Book of Job." In *The Centre and the Periphery: A European Tribute to Walter Brueggemann*. Edited by Jill Middlemas et al., 209–22. Hebrew Bible Monographs 27. Sheffield, UK: Sheffield Phoenix, 2010.

———. *Job 1–20*. WBC 17. Dallas: Word, 1989.

———. "Seven Interesting Things about the Epilogue to Job." *Biblica et Patristica Thoruniensia* 6 (2013) 11–21.

Cogan, Mordechai. *1 Kings: A New Translation with Introduction and Commentary*. AB. New Haven, CT: Yale University Press, 2001.

Cohn, Robert L. *2 Kings*. Berit Olam: Studies in Hebrew Narrative & Poetry. Collegeville, MN: Liturgical, 2000.

———. "Form and Perspective in 2 Kings V." *VT* 33 (1983) 171–84.

Bibliography

Cooper, Alan. "Reading and Misreading the Prologue to Job." *JSOT* 46 (1990) 67–79.

———. "The Sense of the Book of Job." *Prooftexts* 17 (1997) 227–44.

Corr, Charles A. "Should We Incorporate the Work of Elisabeth Kübler-Ross in Our Current Teaching and Practice and, if So, How?" *OMEGA—Journal of Death and Dying* 81 (2019) 1–23.

Davidson, Robert. *The Courage to Doubt: Exploring an Old Testament Theme.* London: SCM, 1983.

Davies, Eryl W. "Walking in God's Ways: The Concept of *Imitatio Dei* in the Old Testament." In *In Search of True Wisdom: Essays in Old Testament Interpretation in Honour of Ronald E. Clements,* edited by Edward Ball, 99–115. JSOTSup 300. Sheffield, UK: Sheffield Academic, 1999.

Davies, Graham I. "The Ethics of Friendship in Wisdom Literature." In *Ethical and Unethical in the Old Testament: God and Humans in Dialogue,* edited by Katharine J. Dell, 135–50. LHBOTS 528. London: T. & T. Clark, 2010.

Davies, John A. "Heptadic Verbal Patterns in the Solomon Narrative of 1 Kings 1–11." *TynBul* 63 (2012) 21–34.

Delitzsch, F. *Biblical Commentary on the Book of Job.* 2nd ed. 2 vols. Edinburgh: T. & T. Clark, 1872–81.

De Rossi, J. B. *Variae lectiones Veteris Testamenti.* 4 vols. Parma, It.: n.p., 1784–88.

Derrida, Jacques. *On Cosmopolitanism and Forgiveness.* Translated by Mark Dooley and Michael Hughes, with a preface by Simon Critchley and Richard Kearney. Thinking in Action. London: Routledge, 2001.

DeVries, Simon J. *1 Kings.* WBC. 2nd ed. Nashville: Thomas Nelson, 2015.

Dhorme, Edouard. *A Commentary on the Book of Job.* Translated by Harold Knight. Nashville: Thomas Nelson, 1984. (Translation of Dhorme, Edouard. *Le livre de Job.* 2nd ed. Paris: Gabalda, 1926.)

Dillmann, August. *Die Bücher Numeri, Deuteronomium und Joshua.* 2nd ed. Kurzgefasstes exegetisches Handbuch zum Alten Testament. Leipzig: Hirzel, 1886.

Downs, David J. *Alms: Charity, Reward and Atonement in Early Christianity.* Waco, TX: Baylor University Press, 2016.

Dozeman, Thomas B. *Exodus.* ECC. Grand Rapids: Eerdmans, 2009.

Driver, S. R. *Notes on the Hebrew Text of the Books of Samuel.* Oxford: Clarendon, 1890.

Driver, S. R., and G. B. Gray. *A Critical and Exegetical Commentary on the Book of Job.* 2 vols. ICC. Edinburgh: T. & T. Clark, 1921.

Elliott-Binns, Leonard E. *The Book of Numbers.* WC 4. London: Methuen, 1927.

Esler, Philip. "Abigail: A Woman of Wisdom and Decisive Action." In *Characters and Characterization in the Book of Samuel,* edited by Keith Bodner and Benjamin J. M. Johnson, 167–82. LHBOTS 669. London: T. & T. Clark, 2020.

Firth, David G. *1 & 2 Samuel.* ApOTC. Nottingham, UK: Apollos, 2009.

Fischer, Georg. "Die Josefgeschichte als Modell für Versöhnung." In *Studies in the Book of Genesis: Literature, Redaction and History,* edited by A Wénin, 243–71. BETL 155. Leuven, Belg.: Peeters, 2001.

Fischer, Irmtraud. "Abigajil: Weisheit und Prophetie in einer Person vereint." In *Auf den Spuren der schriftgelehrten Weisen: Festschrift für Johannes Marböck anlässlich seiner Emeritierung,* edited by Irmtraud Fischer et al, 45–61. Berlin: De Gruyter, 2003.

Fishbane, Michael A. *Biblical Interpretation in Ancient Israel.* Oxford: Clarendon, 1986.

———. *Haftarot.* JPS Commentary. Philadelphia: JPS, 2002.

Bibliography

Fokkelman, Jan P. *The Crossing Fates (I Sam. 13–31 and II Sam. 1)*. Vol. 2 of *Narrative Art and Poetry in the Books of Samuel: A Full Interpretation Based on Stylistic and Structural Analysis*. Assen, Neth.: Van Gorcum, 1986.

Franklin, Benjamin. "On Protection of Towns from Fire." Franklin Papers, Feb. 4, 1734/5. http://franklinpapers.org/framedVolumes.jsp.

Fretheim, Terence E. *Exodus*. Interpretation. Louisville, KY: John Knox, 1991.

———. "Repentance in the Former Prophets." In *Repentance in Christian Theology*, edited by Mark J. Boda and Gordon T. Smith, 25–46. Collegeville, MN: Liturgical, 2006.

Frolov, Serge, and Mikhail Stetckevich. "Repentance in Judges: Assessing the Reassessment." *HS* 60 (2019) 129–40.

Fung, Yiu-Wing. *Victim and Victimizer: Joseph's Interpretation of His Destiny*. JSOTSup 308. Sheffield, UK: Sheffield Academic, 2000.

Galil, Gershon. "The Message of the Book of Kings in Relation to Deuteronomy and Jeremiah." *BSac* 158 (2001) 406–14.

Gane, Roy E. *Cult and Character: Purification Offerings, Day of Atonement, and Theodicy*. University Park: Pennsylvania State University Press, 2005.

———. "Loyalty and Scope of Expiation in Numbers 15." *ZAR* 16 (2010) 249–62.

———. "Numbers 15:22–31 and the Spectrum of Moral Faults." In *Inicios, paradigmas y fundamentos: estudios teológicos y exegéticos en el Pentateuco*, edited by Gerald A. Klingbell, 149–56. Entre Ríos, Arg.: Editorial Universidad Adventista del Plata, 2004.

Gilmour, Rachelle. *Juxtaposition and the Elisha Cycle*. LHBOTS 594. London: T. & T. Clark, 2014.

Gordon, Robert P. *I & II Samuel: A Commentary*. Grand Rapids: Zondervan, 1986.

———. "David's Rise and Saul's Demise: Narrative Analogy in 1 Samuel 24–26." *TynBul* 31 (1980) 37–64.

Gowan, Donald. *The Bible on Forgiveness*. Princeton Theological Monograph 133. Eugene, OR: Pickwick, 2010.

Gray, George B. *A Critical and Exegetical Commentary on Numbers*. ICC. Edinburgh: T. & T. Clark, 1903.

Gray, John. *I & II Kings: A Commentary*. 2nd, rev. ed. OTL. Philadelphia: Westminster, 1976.

Green, Barbara. *How Are the Mighty Fallen? A Dialogical Study of King Saul in 1 Samuel*. JSOTSup 365. London: Sheffield Academic, 2003.

Gross, Carl D. "Notes on the Meaning of Job 16:20." *Bible Translator* 43 (1992) 236–41.

Gunn, David. *The Fate of King Saul: An Interpretation of a Biblical Story*. JSOTSup 14. Sheffield, UK: JSOT, 1980.

Habel, Norman C. *The Book of Job*. OTL. London: SCM, 1985.

Hays, J. Daniel. "Has the Narrator Come to Praise Solomon or to Bury Him? Narrative Subtlety in 1 Kings 1–11." *JSOT* 28 (2003) 149–74.

Hertzberg, Hans Wilhelm. *I & II Samuel: A Commentary*. OTL. London: SCM, 1969.

Hobbs, T. R. *1, 2 Kings*. WBC. Dallas: Word, 1989.

Hoffman, Y. "The Relation between the Prologue and the Speech-Cycles in Job: A Reconsideration." *VT* 31 (1981) 160–70.

House, Paul R. *1, 2 Kings*. NAC 8. Nashville: B&H, 1995.

Houtman, Cornelis. *Exodus*. HCOT. 4 vols. Leuven, Belg.: Peeters, 1993–2002.

Hoyt, JoAnna. "In Defense of YHWH's Unmerited Grace in Judges: A Response to Frolov and Stetckevich." *HS* 61 (2020) 197–211.

———. "Reassessing Repentance in Judges." *BSac* 169 (2012) 143–58.

Jacobs, Mignon. "The Conceptual Dynamics of Good and Evil in the Joseph Story: An Exegetical and hermeneutical Enquiry." *JSOT* 27 (2003) 309–38.

Jastrow, Marcus. *A Dictionary of the Targumim, the Talmud Bavli and Yerushalmi, and the Midrashic Literature.* London: Luzac & Co., 1903.

Jensen, Joseph. *Ethical Dimensions of the Prophets.* Collegeville, MN: Liturgical, 2006.

Jobling, David. *1 Samuel.* Berit Olam: Studies in Hebrew Narrative & Poetry. Collegeville, MN: Liturgical, 1998.

Joseph, Aaron ben. *Sefer ha-Mivchar ve-Tov ha-Mischar: Perush ʿal ha-Torah.* Gozlav: n.p., 1837.

Joüon, P., and T. Muraoka. *A Grammar of Biblical Hebrew.* Rev. ed. SubBi 27. Rome: Pontifical Biblical Institute, 2006.

Kamp, Albert. "The Conceptualization of God's Dwelling Place in 1 Kings 8: A Cognitive Approach." *JSOT* 40 (2016) 415–38.

Kellermann, Diether. "Bemerkungen zum Sündopfergesetz in Num 15,22ff." In *Wort und Geschichte: Festschrift für Karl Elliger zum 70. Geburtsta,* edited by Hartmut Gese and Hans P. Rüger, 107–13. AOAT 18. Neukirchen-Vluyn: Neukirchen, 1973.

Klein, Ralph. *1 Samuel.* WBC. Nashville: Thomas Nelson, 1983.

Knohl, Israel. "The Sin Offering Law in the 'Holiness School' [Numbers 15.22–31]." In *Priesthood and Cult in Ancient Israel,* edited by Gary A. Anderson and Saul M. Olyan, 192–203. JSOTSup 125. Sheffield, UK: JSOT, 1991.

Knoppers, Gary N. "Prayer and Propaganda: Solomon's Dedication of the Temple and the Deuteronomists' Program." *CBQ* 57 (1995) 229–55.

Konstan, David. *Before Forgiveness: The Origins of a Moral Idea.* Cambridge: Cambridge University Press, 2010.

Kugel, James L. *The Great Shift: Encountering God in Biblical Times.* Boston: Houghton Mifflin Harcourt, 2017.

Labuschagne, Casper J. "The Meaning of $b^e y\bar{a}d$ $r\bar{a}m\bar{a}$ in the Old Testament." In *Von Kanaan bis Kerala: Festschrift für Prof. Mag. Dr. J. P. M. van der Ploeg zur Vollendung des siebzigsten Lebensjahrs am 4. Juli 1979 überreicht von Kollegen, Freunden und Schülern,* edited by Wilhelm C. Delsman et al., 143–48. AOAT 211. Neukirchen-Vluyn: Neukirchen, 1983.

Lambdin, Thomas O. *Introduction to Biblical Hebrew.* New York: Scribners, 1971.

Lambert, David A. "Forgiveness and the Question of Interiority in Biblical Tradition." Unpublished paper given at symposium "Remember Their Sin No More? Forgiveness and the Hebrew Bible/Old Testament," Trinity College Dublin, May 11–12, 2018.

———. *How Repentance Became Biblical: Judaism, Christianity, and the Interpretation of Scripture.* New York: Oxford University Press, 2016.

Leithart, Peter J. *1 & 2 Kings.* Brazos Theological Commentary on the Bible. Grand Rapids: Brazos, 2006.

———. "Nabal and His Wine." *JBL* 120 (2001) 525–27.

Levenson, Jon D. "1 Samuel 25 as Literature and as History." *CBQ* 40 (1978) 11–28.

———. "Exodus and Liberation." In *The Hebrew Bible, the Old Testament, and Historical Criticism,* 126–59. Louisville, KY: Westminster John Knox, 1993.

Long, Burke O. *1 Kings with an Introduction to Narrative Literature.* FOTL. Grand Rapids: Eerdmans, 1984.

———. *2 Kings.* FOTL. Grand Rapids: Eerdmans, 1984.

Long, V. Philips. *1 and 2 Samuel: An Introduction and Commentary.* TOTC. Downers Grove, IL: InterVarsity, 2020.

Bibliography

McCarter, P. Kyle., Jr. *I Samuel*. AB. Garden City, NY: Doubleday, 1980.

McConville, J. Gordon. "1 Kings 8:46–53 and the Deuteronomic Hope." In *Reconsidering Israel and Judah: Recent Studies on the Deuteronomic History*, edited by Gary N. Knoppers and J. Gordon McConville, 358–69. Sources for Biblical and Theological Study 8. Winona Lake, IN: Eisenbrauns, 2000.

———. "Forgiveness as Private and Public Act: A Reading of the Biblical Joseph Narrative." *CBQ* 75 (2013) 635–48.

———. "Narrative and Meaning in the Book of Kings." *Biblica* 70 (1989) 31–49.

———. *Judgment and Promise: An Interpretation of the Book of Jeremiah*. Winona Lake, IN: Eisenbrauns, 1993.

McKenzie, Steven L. *1 Kings 16—2 Kings 16*. IECOT. Stuttgart: Kohlhammer, 2019.

Milgrom, Jacob. "Israel's Sanctuary: The Priestly 'Picture of Dorian Gray.'" *RB* 83 (1976) 390–99.

———. *Leviticus 1–16: A New Translation with Introduction and Commentary*. 2nd ed. AB 3. New Haven, CT: Yale University Press, 2009.

———. *Numbers: The Traditional Hebrew Text with the New JPS Translation*. JPS Torah Commentary. Philadelphia: JPS, 1990.

———. "Sin-Offering or Purification-Offering?" *VT* 21 (1971) 237–38.

———. "The Priestly Doctrine of Repentance." *RB* 82 (1975) 186–205.

———. "The Two Pericopes on the Purification Offering." In *The Word of the Lord Shall Go Forth: Essays in Honor of David Noel Freedman in Celebration of His Sixtieth Birthday*, edited by Carol L. Meyers and Michael P. O'Connor, 211–15. ASOR Special Vol. 1. Winona Lake, IN: Eisenbrauns, 1983.

Minas, Anne C. "God and Forgiveness." *Philosophical Quarterly* 27 (1975) 138–50.

Mirguet, Françoise. "What Is an 'Emotion' in the Hebrew Bible? An Experience That Exceeds Most Contemporary Concepts." *BibInt* 24 (2016) 442–65.

Miscall, Peter. *1 Samuel: A Literary Reading*. Bloomington: Indiana University Press, 1986.

Moberly R. W. L. *At the Mountain of God: Story and Theology in Exodus 32–34*. JSOTSup 22. Sheffield, UK: JSOT, 1983.

———. "Review of David A. Lambert, *How Repentance Became Biblical*." *Association of Jewish Studies Review* 41 (2017) 463–66.

Moore, Rick Dale. *God Saves: Lessons from the Elisha Stories*. JSOTSup 95. Sheffield, UK: Sheffield Academic, 1990.

Morgan, Michael L. "Mercy, Repentance, and Forgiveness in Ancient Judaism." In *Ancient Forgiveness: Classical, Judaic, and Christian*, edited by Charles L. Griswold and David Konstan, 137–57. Cambridge: Cambridge University Press, 2011.

Nelson, Richard. *First and Second Kings*. Interpretation. Louisville, KY: John Knox, 1987.

Ngan, Lai Ling Elizabeth. "2 Kings 5." *RevExp* 94 (1997) 589–97.

Nicol, George G. "David, Abigail and Bathsheba, Nabal and Uriah: Transformations within a Triangle." *SJOT* 12 (1998) 130–45.

Noonan, Benjamin J. "High-Handed Sin and the Promised Land: The Rhetorical Relationship between Law and Narrative in Numbers 15." *JSOT* 45 (2020) 79–92.

Noth, Martin. *Das vierte Buch Mose: Numeri*. ATD 7. Göttingen: Vandenhoeck & Ruprecht, 1966.

Novick, Tzvi. "Law and Loss: Response to Catastrophe in Numbers 15." *HTR* 101 (2008) 1–14.

Olivier, J. P. J. סלח. In *NIDOTTE*, 3:259–64.

Olley, John W. "Pharaoh's Daughter, Solomon's Temple and the Palace: Another Look at the Structure of 1 Kings 1–11." *JSOT* 27 (2003) 355–69.

Parker, K. I. "Solomon as Philosopher King? The Nexus of Law and Wisdom in 1 Kings 1–11." *JSOT* 53 (1992) 75–91.

Polzin, Robert. *Samuel and the Deuteronomist: 1 Samuel*. San Francisco: Harper & Row, 1989.

Pope, Marvin. *Job: Introduction, Translation, and Notes*. 3rd ed. AB 15. Garden City, NY: Doubleday, 1980.

Ramban. *Commentary on the Torah: Numbers*. Translated by Charles B. Chave. New York: Shilo, 1975.

Reimer, David J. "The Apocrypha and Biblical Theology: The Case of Interpersonal Forgiveness." In *After the Exile: Essays in Honour of Rex Mason*, edited by John Barton and David J. Reimer, 259–82. Macon, GA: Mercer University Press, 1996.

———. "Interpersonal Forgiveness and the Hebrew Prophets." In *Prophecy and the Prophets in Ancient Israel*, edited by John Day, 81–97. LHBOTS 531. London: Continuum, 2010.

———. "Stories of Forgiveness: Narrative Ethics and the Old Testament." In *Reflection and Refraction: Studies in Biblical Historiography in Honour of A. Graeme Auld*, edited by R. Rezetko, 359–78. VTSup 113. Leiden, Neth.: Brill, 2006.

Rendtorff, Rolf. *Die Gesetze der Priesterschrift: Eine gattungsgeschichtliche Untersuchung*. 2nd ed. Göttingen: Vandenhoeck & Ruprecht, 1963.

———. *Studien zur Geschichte des Opfers im alten Israel*. Neukirchen-Vluyn: Neukirchen, 1967.

Rosenberg, Joel. *King and Kin: Political Allegory in the Hebrew Bible*. Bloomington: Indiana University Press, 1986.

Sarna, Nahum. *Genesis: The Traditional Hebrew Text with the New JPS Translation*. JPS Torah Commentary. Philadelphia: JPS, 1989.

Schmid, Hartmut. *Das Erste Buch der Könige*. Wuppertal, Germ.: Brockhaus, 2000.

Schwartz, Baruch J. "Ezekiel's Dim View of Israel's Restoration." In *The Book of Ezekiel: Theological and Anthropological Perspectives*, edited by Margaret S. Odell and John T. Strong, 43–67. Society of Biblical Literature Symposium 9. Atlanta: SBL, 2000.

Seebass, Horst. *Numeri 10,11—22,1*. BKAT IV/2. Neukirchen-Vluyn: Neuki rchen, 2003.

Shepherd, David J. *King David, Innocent Blood, and Bloodguilt*. Oxford: Oxford University Press, 2023.

Shields, Mary. "A Feast Fit for a King: Food and Drink in the Abigail Story." In *The Fate of King David: The Past and Present of a Biblical Icon*, edited by Tod Linafelt et al., 38–54. LHBOTS 500. New York & London: T. & T. Clark, 2010.

Smith, Duane E. "'Pisser against a Wall': An Echo of Divination in Biblical Hebrew." *CBQ* 72 (2010) 699–717.

Smith, Henry Preserved. *The Books of Samuel*. Edinburgh: T. & T. Clark, 1899.

Spencer, F. Scott, ed. *Mixed Feelings and Vexed Passions: Exploring Emotions in Biblical Literature*. RBS 90. Atlanta: SBL, 2017.

Sprinkle, Preston. "Law and Life: Leviticus 18.5 in the Literary Framework of Ezekiel." *JSOT* 31 (2007) 275–93.

Steinmann, Andrew E. *1 Samuel*. ConcC. Saint Louis: Concordia, 2016.

Stendahl, Krister. "The Apostle Paul and the Introspective Conscience of the West." In *Paul among Jews and Gentiles*, 78–96. Philadelphia: Fortress, 1976.

Stoebe, Hans Joachim. *Das erste Buch Samuelis*. Gütersloh: Mohn, 1973.

Bibliography

Talstra, E. *Solomon's Prayer: Synchrony and Diachrony in the Composition of 1 Kings 8, 14–61.* CBET 3. Kampen, Neth.: Kok Pharos, 1993.

Thigpen, J. Michael. *Divine Motive in the Hebrew Bible: A Comprehensive Survey and Analysis.* Gorgias Biblical Studies 64. Piscataway, NJ: Gorgias, 2015.

Toeg, Arie. "Numbers 15:22–31—Midrash Halakha." [In Hebrew.] *Tarbiz* 43 (1974) 1–10.

Tsumura, David. *The First Book of Samuel.* NICOT. Grand Rapids: Eerdmans, 2007.

Van der Merwe, Christo H. J., et al. *A Biblical Hebrew Reference Grammar.* 2nd ed. London: Bloomsbury T. & T. Clark, 2017.

Van De Wiele, Tara. "Book Review: John Barton, *Ethics in Ancient Israel.*" *Studies in Christian Ethics* 30 (2017) 105–7.

Veijola, Timo. *Die ewige Dynastie: David und die Entstehung seiner Dynastie nach der deuteronomistischen Darstellung.* Helsinki: Suomalainen Tiedeakatemia, 1975.

Ward, Edward. *The Forgiving Husband, and Adulteress Wife: Or a Seasonable Present to the Unhappy Pair in Fanchurch Street.* London: Hills, c. 1708.

Webb, Barry G. *The Book of Judges: An Integrated Reading.* JSOTSup 46. Sheffield, UK: JSOT, 1987.

White, Hugh C. *Narration and Discourse in the Book of Genesis.* Cambridge: Cambridge University Press, 1991.

Widmer, Michael. *Moses, God, and the Dynamics of Intercessory Prayer.* FAT 2/8. Tübingen: Mohr Siebeck, 2004.

———. *Standing in the Breach: An Old Testament Theology and Spirituality of Intercessory Prayer.* Siphrut: Literature and Theology of the Hebrew Scriptures 13. Winona Lake, IN: Eisenbrauns, 2015.

Wittgenstein, Ludwig. *Philosophical Investigations.* Oxford: Blackwell, 1953.

Wray Beal, Lissa M. *1 & 2 Kings.* ApOTC. Nottingham, UK: Apollos, 2014.

Zimmerli, Walther. "Knowledge of God According to the Book of Ezekiel." In *I Am Yahweh,* edited by Walter Brueggemann, translated by Douglas Stott, 29–98. Atlanta: John Knox, 1982.

Name Index

Name Index

Name Index

Sarna, Nahum, 109
Schmid, Hartmut, 54
Schwartz, Baruch J., 37
Seebass, Horst, 29
Shepherd, David J., 3, 5, 47
Shields, Mary, 41
Smith, Duane E., 43
Smith, Henry Preserved, 44
Spencer, F. Scott, 113
Sprinkle, Preston, 79
Steinmann, Andrew E., 46
Stendahl, Krister, 8, 10
Stetckevich, Mikhail, 68, 72
Stoebe, Hans Joachim, 41

Talstra, E., 52, 56, 58
Thigpen, J. Michael, 4, 69, 73–75, 78–80
Toeg, Arie, 3, 23–32, 34–36
Tsumura, David, 46–48

Van De Wiele, Tara, 113
Veijola, Timo, 40

Ward, Edward, 39
Webb, Barry G., 68
White, Hugh C., 105
Widmer, Michael., 11–14
Wittgenstein, Ludwig, 117
Wray Beal, Lissa M., 54, 64

Zimmerli, Walther, 78

Ancient Document Index